Open to the Full Dimension

Open to the Full Dimension

Thomas Merton, Practical Theology,
and Pastoral Practice

DOMINIEK LOOTENS

Foreword by Daniel S. Schipani

WIPF & STOCK · Eugene, Oregon

OPEN TO THE FULL DIMENSION
Thomas Merton, Practical Theology, and Pastoral Practice

Copyright © 2022 Dominiek Lootens. All rights reserved. Except for brief quotations in critical publications or reviews, no part of this book may be reproduced in any manner without prior written permission from the publisher. Write: Permissions, Wipf and Stock Publishers, 199 W. 8th Ave., Suite 3, Eugene, OR 97401.

Wipf & Stock
An Imprint of Wipf and Stock Publishers
199 W. 8th Ave., Suite 3
Eugene, OR 97401

www.wipfandstock.com

PAPERBACK ISBN: 978-1-6667-3506-2
HARDCOVER ISBN: 978-1-6667-9173-0
EBOOK ISBN: 978-1-6667-9174-7

03/04/22

Permissions

The author wishes to thank the following publishers for permission to use the following experts:

Brief quotations throughout the text [285 words] from THE ASIAN JOURNAL OF THOMAS MERTON, by THOMAS MERTON and EDITED BY NAOMI BURTON STONE, et al. Copyright © 1973 by The Merton Legacy Trust. Reprinted by permission of New Directions.

Brief quotations throughout the text [1.143 words] from CONTEMPLATION IN A WORLD OF ACTION, by THOMAS MERTON. Copyright © 1971 by the Merton Legacy Trust. Reprinted by permission of Doubleday.

Brief quotations throughout the text [376 words] from THE HIDDEN GROUND OF LOVE: LETTERS ON RELIGIOUS EXPERIENCE AND SOCIAL CONCERNS, by THOMAS MERTON and EDITED BY WILLIAM H. SHANNON. Copyright © 1985 by The Merton Legacy Trust. Reprinted by permission of Farrar, Straus & Giroux.

Brief quotations throughout the text [261 words] from THE INNER EXPERIENCE: NOTES ON CONTEMPLATION, by THOMAS MERTON and EDITED BY WILLIAM H. SHANNON. Copyright © 2003 by The Merton Legacy Trust. Reprinted by permission of HarperSanFrancisco.

Brief quotations throughout the text [298 words] from MYSTICS & ZEN MASTERS, by THOMAS MERTON. Copyright © 1967 by The Abbey of Gethsemani. Reprinted by permission of Farrar, Straus & Giroux.

Brief quotations throughout the text [41 words] from RAIDS ON THE UNSPEAKABLE, by THOMAS MERTON. Copyright © 1966 by The Abbey of Gethsemani. Reprinted by permission of New Directions.

Brief quotations throughout the text [1.109 words] from THE SPRINGS OF CONTEMPLATION: A RETREAT AT THE ABBEY OF GETHSEMANI, by THOMAS MERTON and EDITED BY JANE MARIE RICHARDSON. Copyright © 1992 by The Merton Legacy Trust. Reprinted by permission of Farrar, Straus & Giroux.

Brief quotations throughout the text [158 words] from THOUGHTS IN SOLITUDE, by THOMAS MERTON. Copyright © 1958 by The Abbey of Gethsemani. Reprinted by permission of Farrar, Straus & Cudahy and Curtis Brown Ltd.

Brief quotations throughout the text [273 words] from A VOW OF CONVERSATION: JOURNALS 1964–1965, by THOMAS MERTON and EDITED BY NAOMI BURTON STONE. Copyright © 1988 by The Merton Legacy Trust. Reprinted by permission of Farrar, Straus & Giroux.

Previously unpublished letter from Thomas Merton to Cardinal Suenens, Sept. 10, 1964. Copyright © 2022 by The Trustees of The Merton Legacy Trust. Used by permission of the Trustees.

Contents

Foreword by Daniel S. Schipani | ix
Acknowledgments | xiii
Introduction: Reading Thomas Merton | xvii

1. Thomas Merton and Catholic Chaplaincy in a Multi-Faith Context | 1
2. Thomas Merton, Migration, and Practical Theology | 17
3. Thomas Merton and Pastoral Supervision | 29
4. Thomas Merton, Natural Contemplation, and Orthodox Pastoral Theology | 53
5. Thomas Merton and Septima Clark on the Civil Rights Movement and Adult Education | 76
6. Thomas Merton and the Education of Social Justice Allies | 88

Appendix: Letter of Thomas Merton to Cardinal Suenens | 97
Bibliography | 101
Index | 111

Foreword

DOMINIEK LOOTENS ASSERTS THAT Thomas Merton can be a focus of today's conversations in practical theology, and a dialogue partner in discussions on contemplative chaplaincy, theological reflection, pastoral care and art, self and spiritual maturity, and mystical-prophetic approaches in the field. This book develops and illustrates that proposal systematically, insightfully, and fruitfully. The author succeeds in introducing Merton to pastoral practitioners while also disclosing the contours of his contemplative-prophetic approach, which stems from his own practice of pastoral supervision, education, and active participation in interreligious endeavors.

Several features of the text can be highlighted, beginning with the author's invitation to pastoral practitioners to discover for themselves the comprehensive relevance of Merton's legacy for their work. In that way, the book can function as a helpful Merton primer that elicits further interdisciplinary engagement. Manifold quotes from a wide variety of writings can thus inspire the readers in their ongoing work of doing practical theology. Lootens also shows us how to read and appropriate Merton's contributions specifically within the domains and settings of specialized vocational practices such as hospital chaplaincy, adult education, and justice and peacemaking. His focus on the cooperation between

Foreword

Christian and Muslim chaplains is particularly noteworthy. It is also significant that Lootens invites the reader to engage in dialogue with Orthodox pastoral theologians.

Another significant feature of this book is its detailed, clear, careful documentation of the author's approach to pastoral and practical theology. Dominiek Lootens has developed a three-way hermeneutical method that engages Thomas Merton's work and thought in dialectical interaction with Lootens's own and with the contributions of diverse authors whose concerns complement and further Merton's. The epistemic import of such critical and constructive practice is very significant. To put it in simple terms, Lootens doesn't simply "follow" Thomas Merton; rather, he "re-creates" his manifold contribution.

This book is therefore, a fine illustration of doing pastoral and practical theology. The author demonstrates apostolic commitment facing a number of challenges within specific social contexts and institutional settings. He then engages in interpretive analysis with interdisciplinary lenses. The *contemplative* (or *mystical*) dimension of his approach is particularly, although not exclusively, evident in these descriptive-empirical and hermeneutic phases of his reflection. His (Christian faith-grounded) normative framework is of course evident in terms of freedom, peace with justice, care and overall wellbeing, life-giving and community-building. Finally, the pragmatic orientation towards effective—that is, competent and faithful—praxis completes the process. The *prophetic* dimensions of Lootens's practical-theological approach is especially, although not exclusively, evident in the normative and strategic phases of his practical theology.

In sum, this book is a timely resource to be welcome during this pandemic time. Our fundamental human vulnerability has been exposed in new ways together with specific, contextually situated vulnerability and suffering correlated with unjust socioeconomic and political systems. Chaplaincy and other caregiving settings, migration, the environment, human and civil rights, education and pastoral supervision, are some of the key areas that can

Foreword

be further illumined and engaged in light of Thomas Merton, as recreated by Dominiek Lootens.

Daniel S. Schipani, Dr. Psy., Ph.D.
Professor Emeritus,
Anabaptist Mennonite
Biblical Seminary

Acknowledgments

FIRST AND FOREMOST I would like to thank the pastoral practitioners and practical theologians whom I had the opportunity to meet during my practice as a pastoral supervisor and educator. The motivation to write this book is based on my cooperation with them.

I would like to thank Doris Nauer, who has encouraged me to pursue and complete this project. My good friend and mentor Daniel S. Schipani has helped me to take my perspective as practical theologian and pastoral supervisor seriously in interpreting the life and work of Thomas Merton. I sincerely thank him for writing such a wonderful foreword. A sincere thank you to my dear friend Candace Moser, who did the proofreading with much dedication and enthusiasm.

I would like to thank Christine Bochen, Mike A. Brennan, Roger Burggraeve, James G. R. Cronin, Petra Döll, Zehra Erşahin, Willy Eurlings, Fiona Gardner, David Golemboski, Kathleen Greider, Cassidy Hall, Ursula Harfst, Jane Heckles, Johanna Hessemer, Marianne Hieb, Daniel P. Horan, Johan Hovelynck, Eberhard Jost, Edward K. Kaplan, Deborah P. Kehoe, Laura

Acknowledgments

Knäbel, Susan Kolac-Lang, Alan Kolp, Sarah Kothe, Stephanie Krauch, Agnes Lanfermann, Alexander Lang, Sybryn Leirs, Olga Lossky-Laham, Alexander Letz, Steffi Manger, Mark Meade, Luc Meeusen, Josh Morris, Margret Noltensmeier, Frances Norwood, Peter Noss, Anthony Nuccio, Patrick F. O'Connell, Gordon Oyer, Michael Paterson, Paul Pearson, Neil Pembroke, Michael P. Plekon, Chris Pramuk, Paul Pynkoski, Marcella Raggio, Jenny Ratigan, Jim Ratigan, Daniel Saudek, Harald Schwalbe, Meena Sharify-Funk, Chani Smith, Jill Snodgrass, Susanna Snyder, Marie Somerville, Dennis Stammer, Dewi M. Suharjanto, Kathleen W. Tarr, Klaus Temme, Bonnie Thurston, Martin van Ditzhuyzen, Judith Valente, George Varughese, Johannes Volker Schmidt, Martin Walton, Tobias Müller, and Monica Weis for their interest, feedback, friendship and support.

It is a unique gift that the Legacy Trust gave me permission to include the previously unpublished letter from Thomas Merton to the Belgian Cardinal Suenens. This letter has helped me to keep in mind that I look at Merton from a Belgian and European perspective.

Several of the chapters that follow contain material previously published as lectures or articles. They have been rethought and adapted for his book. I thank the editors and publishers for publishing this earlier material. Giving these lectures and writing these articles helped me to find my voice as a Merton scholar.

"Thomas Merton and the Vocation of Peacemaking. Catholic Chaplaincy in a Multi-Faith Context." In *Navigating Religious Difference in Spiritual Care and Counseling*, edited by Jill L. Snodgrass, 135–49. Claremont, CA: Claremont, 2019.

"Thomas Merton and the Displaced Person: A Response to Susanna Snyder." In *Where Are We? Pastoral Environments and Care for Migrants: Intercultural and Interreligious Perspectives*, edited by Daniel Schipani et al., 183–94. Düsseldorf, Germany: SIPCC, 2018.

"Aandacht voor Spiritualiteit: Thomas Merton en Pastorale Supervisie." In *Pastorale Supervisie: Een handboek*, by Jane Leach and Michael Paterson, in cooperation with Dominiek Lootens, 257–76. Oud-Turnhout: Gompel & Svacina, 2019.

Acknowledgments

"Thomas Merton and the Spiritual Roots of Protest: Educational Reflections on the Peacemaker Retreat." *The Merton Seasonal* 42 (2017) 12–16.

Above all, I would like to thank my *Kochanie* in life, my wife Nina. Her belief and support for my work have been a constant inspiration. I dedicate this book to Nina's father and my mother, both of whom passed away while I was working on it. I humbly thank them for what they did to help me become the man I am today.

Dominiek Lootens
Advent, 2021

Introduction
Reading Thomas Merton

DURING HIS LIFETIME, THOMAS Merton (1915–68) was very prolific as a writer. I started reading him, like many people, by coincidence. The first book I came across was an older Dutch version of his edited journal *Conjectures of a Guilty Bystander*.[1] I learned from this book how in Merton's life the contemplative and the prophetic were strongly related. I was hooked on the writing style of that book and since then, Merton has become a favorite conversation partner.

There have been several ways in which I have read the writings of Thomas Merton. The first way of reading him was for pleasure. On January 27, 1966, in a letter to his close friend John Wu, Merton writes ironically about his own writings:

> Usually my writings are good for putting people to sleep, but you are prejudiced . . . don't read anything that robs you of sleep: sleep is better than reading.[2]

---

1. Merton, *Conjectures*.
2. Quoted in Serrán-Pagán y Fuentes, *Merton & the Tao*, 322.

Introduction

Funny enough, I recognize what Merton is talking about. For the past ten years or so, I have loved reading Merton in the evening, just before I go to bed. I have read the edited versions of his journals as well as other books, especially those Merton wrote in the last decade of his life. Reading a few pages helps me relax, reflect on the day, let go of what happened, and enjoy his well-written texts. At that point of the day, I don't read him to do research. It is an associative read where his thoughts and experiences get into dialogue with my daily life. And indeed, I agree that I fall asleep more easily afterwards.

The second way I read Thomas Merton was to appreciate him as a spiritual writer. In 1961, Merton taught a pastoral course on spiritual direction at Gethsemani Abbey. During this course, he introduced his students to *lectio divina*.[3] I learned from the poet and Merton scholar Susan McCaslin, that one can apply this method of *lectio divina* not only to the Bible but also to Merton's writings.[4] As an experiment, McCaslin read some of his poems in this way. In my own experience, Merton's spiritual writings, especially *Thoughts in Solitude* and *New Seeds of Contemplation*, have such an evocative character that they invite me to read them using this meditative method.[5] Thanks to this way of reading Merton's books, I have developed a broader view of *lectio divina*.

The third way was to become acquainted with the way scholars write about Merton. There is a significant international and interdisciplinary community of Merton scholars. They have done critical analysis of his writings. They played an important role in helping me situate Merton in the history of the Catholic Church and the context of the twentieth century. Reading their research has helped me to better understand the strengths and limits of Merton's writings.

Through reading Merton, especially his journals and letters, I came to know him not only as a contemplative writer and prophet,

---

3. Merton, *Introduction to Mysticism*, 332–40.
4. McCaslin, "Transformative Solitudes."
5. Merton, *Thoughts in Solitude*. Merton, *New Seeds*.

Introduction

but also as a pastoral practitioner. Before I say more about this book, let me give some examples of his pastoral ministry.

PASTORAL MINISTRY OF THOMAS MERTON

On September 10, 1965, Merton wrote a letter to the Belgian Cardinal Suenens.[6] Together with Merton's close friend, Loretto Sister Mary Luke Tobin, Cardinal Suenens discussed the pastoral task of active congregations of sisters in the context of a changing world, at the Second Vatican Council.[7] Merton wrote a letter to the Cardinal, supporting him in his task and giving him his vision for the pastoral ministry of contemplative monks. This letter has a strong autobiographical character. Merton begins his reflections with a reference to his experience of writing books and having ecumenical contacts with retreatants in the monastery. He emphasizes that the pastoral ministry of a contemplative monk can be fruitful only when it is an integral part of his life as a monk. Prayer, study, and solitude play a central part. At the same time, monks have other duties within the monastery. From 1951 until 1965, Merton was responsible for the education of young monks within the monastery, first as master of scholastics and later as master of novices. In this capacity, he was also their spiritual director. Merton scholar Lawrence Cunningham has argued that one of the reasons Merton's writings appeal so much to us today is that they are based on his years of experience as a man of prayer, educator, and spiritual director within the monastery.[8]

In his letter to Suenens, Merton explains what pastoral ministry a contemplative monk might take on. He begins his overview with writing. He stresses in his typical ironic style that a monk should only write if he has the talent for it and if he has something to say. Works of sacred art and music could also be an option if a monk has a talent for them. A monk may also have a vocation for

6. See Appendix.
7. McCloskey, "More Than a Footnote."
8. Cunningham, *Thomas Merton and Monastic Vision*, 208.

Introduction

scholarship and research which can be seen, directly or indirectly, as a kind of pastoral ministry. One of the central pastoral tasks of a contemplative monk is likely to be preaching at retreats and offering spiritual direction, for example, to pastoral practitioners and artists. As a final possibility, he mentions a limited amount of teaching and lecturing in the context of retreat centers, other monasteries, colleges and secular universities.

In reading Thomas Merton's published journals, especially *Dancing in the Water of Life*, which contains his diary from August 1963 to December 1965, I realized that Merton practiced the different types of pastoral ministry that he describes in his letter to Cardinal Suenens.[9] This diary also helps us to see how he concretized his task as novice master and spiritual director.

It is clear that Merton enjoyed working with the novices and was concerned with their welfare. He developed a variety of methods to educate them in an attractive way. Not only did he lecture them in art and on writers like Simone Weil, but he also gave them randomly copied Bible fragments as Christmas gifts, played records (by the famous Belgian nun *Soeur Sourire*!), took nature walks and worked in the forest with them.

As he began to spend more time in the hermitage, he walked up and down to the monastery to teach and provide spiritual direction. He was involved in the selection of candidates for the monastery and sometimes had to intervene in crisis situations. He mentions that one of the novices suffered a psychotic breakdown.

Regarding his pastoral ministry, he reflects on the articles and books he has written and the amount of letters he has to write. In a famous letter to Pope John XXIII, Merton described his writing of letters as a ministry of friendship.[10] In 1964, he was doing research on the Voyage of St. Brendan which resulted in a well-researched article on pilgrimage and Celtic monasticism.[11] In that same year, he prepared an exhibition of his calligraphies at the Catherine Spalding College in Louisville. During that period of his life, he

9. Merton, *Dancing in the Water*.
10. Merton, *Life in Letters*, xi–xii.
11. Weis, *Thomas Merton and Celts*, 44–65.

Introduction

regularly held retreats for seminary students from various Protestant theological institutions. He was giving lectures in the mother house of the Loretto sisters and in the fall of 1964, he organized the famous retreat for peace activists.

THOMAS MERTON AND PRACTICAL THEOLOGY

Within the field of practical theology, Thomas Merton is part of today's discussions. Merton is a discussion partner in reflections on contemplative chaplaincy, theological reflection, pastoral care and art, self and spiritual maturity, and mystical-prophetic approaches to practical theology.

Rev. Marc Clayton is a chaplain at Martin House Children's Hospice in West Yorkshire, UK. Reading Merton as a spiritual author helped him create a concept for his pastoral ministry. He has developed a contemplative approach to his work with children.[12]

Practical theologians have an appreciation for Thomas Merton as an autobiographical author. To support UK students, scholars and practitioners in their skills as practical theologians, Elaine Graham, Heather Walton, and Frances Ward have created a handbook with different methods of theological reflection.[13] In the sourcebook accompanying this handbook Graham, Walton, and Ward have included a fragment of *The Seven Storey Mountain*, Merton's autobiography.[14] For them, Merton can be seen as an inspiration for studying "living human documents."

Australian researcher Terry A. Veling has developed a narrative approach to practical theology. He draws on the European hermeneutical tradition, Jewish mysticism, Emanuel Levinas and wisdom speakers (poets and songwriters). He also refers to *The Seven Storey Mountain* and sees it as a classic in narrative reflection.[15]

---

12. Clayton, "Contemplative Chaplaincy?"; Clayton, "Hidden Wholeness."

13. Graham et al., *Theological Reflection: Methods*.

14. Graham et al., *Theological Reflection: Sources*, 56–63. Merton, *Seven Storey Mountain*.

15. Veling, *Practical Theology*, 96.

Introduction

Neil Pembroke is an Australian practical theologian who has done significant interdisciplinary research on Thomas Merton.[16] According to the spiritual scholar Philip F. Sheldrake, one of the biggest contributions of Merton is his theology of the self.[17] Based on a narrative approach, Pembroke uses the famous distinction Merton makes between the false and the real self to reflect on spiritual maturity.[18] He also brings Thomas Merton and Simone Weil into dialogue to reflect on a spirituality of self-emptying.[19]

Claire Wolfteich, a US researcher, has convincingly demonstrated the importance of bringing practical theology into dialogue with spiritual studies.[20] She mentions Merton as a historical figure who could inspire such a dialogue.[21] Renowned theologian and spiritual scholar David Tracy has argued that Thomas Merton is a pioneer in a mystical-prophetic approach to spirituality.[22] At the same time, Tracy has argued that there is need for a mystical-prophetic approach to practical theology.[23] Wolfteich has developed such an approach, based on the writings of Michel de Certeau.[24]

In this book, I take up the suggestion of Claire Wolfteich and David Tracy. I develop a mystical-prophetic approach for my practice as pastoral supervisor and educator with Thomas Merton as conversation partner. In accordance with Merton, I will use "contemplative" and "mystical" interchangeably in this book.[25]

---

16. Pembroke, "Merton's True Self."
17. Sheldrake, "Contemplation and Social Transformation." Sheldrake, *Explorations in Spirituality*, 124–137.
18. Pembroke, *Moving toward Spiritual Maturity*, 102–11.
19. Pembroke, "Two Spiritualities."
20. Wolfteich, "Animating Questions."
21. Wolfteich, "Spirituality," 331.
22. Tracy, "Recent Catholic Spirituality."
23. Tracy, "Correlational Model Revisited."
24. Wolfteich, "Practices of Unsaying."
25. Merton, *Contemplation in a World*, 172–73.

Introduction

THE APPROACH OF THIS BOOK

A central aim of this book is to introduce Merton to pastoral practitioners so that they can discover for themselves how relevant he can be in their professional lives

For two decades, I worked as a pastoral supervisor and pastoral educator. Within the context of Caritas Flanders, I was responsible for the continuing professional education of Catholic healthcare chaplains. As vice president of SIPCC, the Society for Intercultural Pastoral Care and Counseling, I was involved in the preparation and moderating of international and interreligious seminars for pastoral practitioners and practical theologians. Since 2018, I have been working in Germany as an adult educator and community worker in the diocese of Limburg, with a focus on ecology, natural sciences, city development and congregational change.

Since 2011, Merton has been a regular conversation partner for me. Reading him has helped me to think more broadly and deeply about my professional life. While researching Merton, I have given talks and made new friends at General Meetings of the International Thomas Merton Society.

I have chosen to use my professional background as a pastoral practitioner for the starting point of this book. From this specific perspective, I have approached the writings of Thomas Merton. It is important for a pastoral practitioner to be skilled in theological reflection. My colleague, Jane Leach, who works as a practical theologian and pastoral supervisor in the United Kingdom, has developed a method for theological reflection that has inspired my approach to this book.[26] She poses five questions that can be helpful for pastoral practitioners to theologically reflect upon concrete professional experiences in groups or individually.

1. Whose voices can you hear (and whose are silent)?
2. What are the wider issues implicit here?
3. What are your own hearts saying?
4. What does the Christian tradition have to say?

26. Leach, "Pastoral Theology as Attention."

5. What, in the light of all this, is the mission of the church, and within that, your task, here and now?

I mentioned already that Merton himself had considerable experience in pastoral ministry. In reading his journals, letters, spiritual writings, books and essays, I have discovered that he was a pioneer in theological reflection. He asked himself questions that we, as professionals, must also ask if we are to work responsibly in today's global context.

It is not possible for me as a pastoral practitioner and researcher to dialogue with Thomas Merton in a naïve way.[27] In the epilogue of her classic study on Merton's theology of the self, Merton scholar Anne E. Carr stresses the importance of a critical approach.

> In addition to the important insights which Merton achieved and that mark his work as the most influential and widely read American religious thinker of our time, we must note the weaknesses which his best commentators have pointed out. These critiques represent the grain of salt with which Merton's writings must always be approached, the critical thought that would avoid a cult of mere adulation and that Merton himself would most appreciate in his readers. It has been said that Mertons's spiritual theology is increasingly elitist and eccentric, obsessive and esoteric, and above all, eclectic. And there is some truth to all these claims.[28]

An important aspect that needs to be addressed in this introduction is Merton's use of exclusive language: "Merton had yet to apply more inclusive language, with his constant use of both gender exclusivity (typically using 'men' and 'man') and dated language when discussing Black men and women (his frequent use of 'negro')."[29] It is not enough to explain that such language was standard in Merton's time and then let the topic rest. I agree with Merton scholar Daniel Horan that it is important to point out

27. Holder, "Problem with Spiritual Classics"; Miles, *Practicing Christianity*; Weaver, "Conjectures."
28. Carr, *Search for Wisdom*, 146.
29. Hall, Review of *Thomas Merton for Our Time*, 28.

Introduction

Merton's use of exclusive language and to use this observation as opportunity to reflect on the systemic roots of different kinds of exclusion within our everyday lives and society at large.[30]

The research of the historical theologian Margaret Miles has helped me especially find my own approach in writing this book. She has developed a hermeneutical method based on Martha Nussbaum. Miles calls her approach "Reading for life."[31]

> Reading for life is different than reading for entertainment. It is also different than reading to understand the author's communication. It is not academic reading, assigned reading. Reading for life desperately seeks suggestions—clues—about how to get what I most deeply long for.[32]

Miles showed me a way to maintain my initial enthusiasm for this favorite author of mine, Thomas Merton, and to simultaneously use my reflective and theological skills in writing this book.

Thomas Merton once wrote in his journal, that his vocation was reading. He read out of necessity.[33] In his reading of classical and contemporary authors, he desperately wanted to find clues for living a joyful, generous and responsible life as a monk and pastoral practitioner.

Pastoral practitioners can use this book to discover the relevance of Merton's work for their practice. There are two ways to read this publication. The first is to focus on the Merton quotes and to read them separately as an aid for theological reflection. The second way is to read them in the context of the different chapters in this book.

---

30. Horan, *Thomas Merton for Our Time*.
31. Miles, *Reading for Life*.
32. Miles, *Recollections*, 76.
33. Merton, *Dancing in the Water*, 124.

Introduction

STRUCTURE OF THIS BOOK

In the first chapter, I reflect on Catholic healthcare chaplaincy in the technological environment of hospitals in today's Belgian pluralistic context. Based on my reading of Thomas Merton, I invite Catholic chaplains to reflect on their position and to engage in interfaith chaplaincy. The initial impetus for this chapter was my reading of *The Springs of Contemplation*, an edited version of two retreats Merton led for contemplative prioresses in 1967 and 1968.[34]

During his lifetime, Merton wrote many reviews.[35] The second chapter is based on this writing practice and on his edited journal, *The Asian Journal*.[36] This chapter offers a review of Susanna Snyder's excellent book, *Asylum-Seeking, Migration and Church*.[37] I want to explore what it means to work responsibly as a pastoral practitioner and practical theologian in a context of migration.

The third chapter is based on my work as a trainer of pastoral supervisors. The basic reading for this chapter was Merton's book *Contemplation in a World of Action*.[38] I take the APSE[39] definition of pastoral supervision and based on my reading of Merton, I describe this pastoral practice as attention, transformation, and an exercise in nonviolence.

Since we moved to Germany, I have been focusing on ecological issues in my work as a pastoral practitioner. In the fourth chapter, I introduce Merton as an animal theologian. This chapter has a more historical character. Merton was well acquainted with the research of a group of orthodox theologians who were working at Saint-Sergius in Paris. The basic reading I used was Merton's pastoral course on spiritual direction, *An Introduction to Christian Mysticism*.[40] I focus on his interpretation of Evagrius and

34. Merton, *Springs of Contemplation*.
35. Weis, "Ishi Means Man."
36. Merton, *Asian Journal*.
37. Snyder, *Asylum-Seeking*.
38. Merton, *Contemplation in a World*.
39. APSE: Association of Pastoral Supervisors and Educators (UK).
40. Merton, *Introduction to Mysticism*.

Introduction

Maximus the Confessor. I bring him into dialogue with two orthodox pastoral theologians, Kyprian Kern and Elisabeth Behr-Sigel. Merton probably did not know them, but they were also working at Saint-Sergius.

In reading his journal, *Dancing in the Water of Life*, I discovered how Merton reflected on his role as a social justice ally within the context of the civil rights movement.[41] This diary was written at a time when civil rights marches and protests were taking place. One of the central figures in this movement was the citizenship educator Septima Clark (1898–1987). In the fifth chapter, I reflect on my role as pastoral educator within a context of racism and white privilege. I do this by bringing Clark and Merton into dialogue with each other.

The final chapter is based on my practice of training Catholic healthcare chaplains as social justice allies. The starting point for this chapter is the research of the Merton scholar, Gordon Oyer. He has written a wonderful book on the famous peacemaker retreat that took place at Gethsemani Abbey in the fall of 1964.[42] I explore what I can learn as a pastoral educator from this retreat.

---

41. Merton, *Dancing in the Water*.
42. Oyer, *Pursuing Spiritual Roots*.

1

Thomas Merton and Catholic Chaplaincy in a Multi-Faith Context

THOMAS MERTON (1915–68) WAS a famous Trappist monk, spiritual writer, pacifist, poet, and social activist. He died more than fifty years ago on December 10, 1968. To commemorate his life and writings, I focus in this first chapter on two of his retreats. My aim is to illustrate how relevant his work still is, especially for Catholic chaplains working in today's high-tech, multi-faith, healthcare context.

THOMAS MERTON: A SHORT BIOGRAPHY

Thomas Merton was born on January 31, 1915 in Prades, in the South of France. His parents were artists who met each other in Paris. Owen Merton, his father, came originally from New Zealand, and his mother, Ruth Jenkins, was a citizen of the United States. They both had Protestant roots. When Thomas Merton was six, his mother died of cancer. Ten years later, his father died because of a brain tumor. After a turbulent time as a student at

Open to the Full Dimension

Cambridge, in 1935 Merton started studying English literature at Columbia University in New York. In 1939 he converted to Catholicism. After finishing his studies, he worked as a lecturer in English literature at St. Bonaventure University. In 1941 he entered the Trappist monastery of Gethsemani in Kentucky. Supported by his superiors, Merton published his autobiography in 1948, *The Seven Story Mountain*, which became an international bestseller.[1]

From 1955 till 1965 Thomas Merton was master of novices in the abbey. In that period he thought deeply about the role of education and about monastic reform. He also organized several ecumenical retreats.

Thanks to his letters, the many visitors whom he received in the abbey, and the travels he undertook at the end of his life, Merton was very well aware of what was happening in the United States and around the world. The list of people with whom he was in contact is impressive and included Daniel Berrigan, Dom Helder Camara, Ernesto Cardenal, Dorothy Day, Katherine de Hueck Doherty, Erich Fromm, Thích Nhất Hạnh, Abraham Joshua Heschel, Dalai Lama, Jacques Maritain, Louis Massignon, Henry Miller, Czeslaw Milosz, Sayyed Hossein Nasr, Henri Nouwen, Victoria Ocampo, Boris Pasternak, Pope John XXIII, Pope Paul VI, Rosemary Radford Ruether, and Evelyn Waugh.

In 1965 Merton received permission to live as a hermit near the abbey. In 1968 he traveled to Asia and visited religious places in India, Sri Lanka, and Thailand. On December 10, 1968 Merton died in Bangkok after giving a lecture at a conference for superiors of religious orders.

Today Thomas Merton is best known as a spiritual author. People who are more familiar with his work know that in his later writings he devoted himself strongly to social themes: interfaith and intra-religious dialogue, poverty and social exclusion, peace and nonviolence, literature and art, ecology and technology.

In December 1967, during one of the retreats he gave for a group of contemplative prioresses,[2] Merton said the following

---

1. Merton, *Seven Storey Mountain*.
2. Merton organized two retreats for this group of prioresses, one in

Thomas Merton and Catholic Chaplaincy in a Multi-Faith Context

about reading the Bible: "It's wonderful how you can take text after text, and the same text over and over again, and just apply them to different situations, how much light comes out of them in the new situation."[3] Merton of course never wrote any holy scripture himself. Nevertheless, in my experience, the key he offered to reading the Bible can also be applied to the texts that he wrote in the last decade of his life.

In this chapter I will focus on the edited texts of the two retreats Merton organized for the group of contemplative prioresses. These texts serve as a lens for viewing Catholic health care chaplaincy practice in Belgium and making a call for revised practice. The chapter starts with a short clarification of today's Belgian context. I then present three common responses by Catholic chaplains to this changing context. Several fragments from Merton's text offer insights for viewing these three common responses and demonstrating the promising nature of the third response. These fragments invite Catholic chaplains to realize their vocation as interfaith chaplains. Merton supports chaplains in their commitment to become peacemakers, even while they are working within a high-tech, multi-faith healthcare context.

A BRIEF LOOK AT THE BELGIAN CONTEXT

The hot topic in European society today is the so-called refugee crisis. Liberal and conservative politicians alike stress that migrants have to behave as "normal" people, they have to accept the values associated with European history. This is especially true for migrants with a Muslim background. One basic assumption is that Europe is ethically and politically more evolved than the Muslim world. In Europe the "Muslim world is still often seen as a monolithic, unchanging, under-developed, violent, anti-democratic

---

December 1967 and one in May 1968. The edited texts of both retreats can be found in Merton, *Springs of Contemplation*. For a critical discussion of the editing of the original recordings of the retreats, see O'Connell, Review *of Merton on Contemplation*.

3. Merton, *Springs of Contemplation*, 121.

space as a direct result of the perceived characteristics of Islam."[4] Although some secular thinkers in Belgium admit that Muslims have the right to bring their religion to the public fore, they fear that they will use this right to undermine Western democratic values. According to Loobuyck "the enemy of the secular state is not the religion, but the (fundamentalist) religion and other ideologies in so far as they do not accept the fundamental rights and principles of liberal democracy."[5]

The percentage of Muslims in Belgian society is increasing, and this is something that healthcare professionals have to take into account.[6] From a secular perspective, Loobuyck argues that they should learn how to deal with such a religious tradition in a professional way: "You need a professional attitude to deal with this diversity and with your own philosophy of life."[7]

If you look at the healthcare context in Belgium today, especially hospitals, you find much stress on medical innovation and managerial efficiency. These two developments go hand-in-hand. There is the belief that progress in the medical sciences will make healthcare less costly. All disciplines are pushed to take up their responsibility to become more evidence-based and efficient. According to Loobuyck "there reigns a systemic distrust which implies that you constantly have to prove yourself, make dashes at the number of beds you have done and conversations you have had. On top of that, there is an inflation of evaluation procedures, which often are based on criteria that have little or nothing to do with the profession you practice."[8]

---

4. Haynes, "Constructions of European Identity," 52.

5. Loobuyck, *Seculiere Samenleving*, 242.

6. In a recent Study, the Pew Research Center estimates that 55 percent of the Belgian population identify themselves as Christian, 38 percent as religiously unaffiliated (Pew Research Center, "Being Christian"). According to another study of the Pew Research Center, 7.6 percent identify as Muslim. In 2050, in a medium migration scenario, possibly 15.1 percent of the population will identify as Muslim (Pew Research Center, "Europe's Muslim Population").

7. Quoted in Polis, "Kleur van Zorg," 27.

8. Quoted in Polis, "Kleur van Zorg," 27.

DEVELOPMENTS IN CATHOLIC CHAPLAINCY IN BELGIUM

Looking at the history of healthcare chaplaincy in Europe, a lot has changed in the last few decades. Twenty years ago I started to work in Belgium as a pastoral educator and supervisor in the Catholic Diocese of Antwerp. In those days the majority of chaplains were priests and people from religious orders. Now the vast majority of Catholic chaplains are lay people.

Working for Caritas Flanders as a white, male, heterosexual, Catholic layperson, I had the opportunity to write a dissertation on chaplaincy education.[9] My position as an educator and pastoral supervisor enabled me to build relationships with professionals, managers, and academics in Belgium and abroad.

Through the years it became more and more clear to me that it is not so easy to be a Catholic chaplain in today's healthcare context. People who do this kind of work often feel marginalized.[10] Management and other disciplines ask why chaplains are still necessary in a secular context. Patients seem not to be interested to talk about religion, they just want to get better. Chaplaincy is very costly, and chaplains are unable to present any reliable results. At the same time, looking from a multi-faith perspective, I became more and more aware of the fact that Catholic chaplains in Belgium are still in a privileged position. Catholic chaplains are able work in Catholic and public hospitals. Only a small number of Protestant chaplains and Humanist counselors work in public hospitals. A few Muslim chaplains work on a voluntarily basis, mostly in public hospitals.[11]

---

9. Lootens, *Kraft der Phantasie*.
10. Norwood, "Ambivalent Chaplain."
11. In his study on young organized Muslims in Brussels and London, Pędziwiatr writes: "Among other issues that were mentioned by my interviewees less frequently in the context of unequal treatment of Islam as a recognized faith, were inter alia the right to have state-paid chaplains in prisons and hospitals." Pędziwiatr, *New Muslim Elites*, 253.

Open to the Full Dimension

CHAPLAINS' RESPONSES TO THE CHANGING HEALTHCARE CONTEXT

Catholic chaplains react differently to Belgium's changing healthcare context, yet many respond in one of the following three ways.[12] The first response is to assert themselves as real professionals. The second response entails concentrating exclusively on the unique characteristics of pastoral care. The third response is to commit themselves to interfaith chaplaincy, based on a contemplative perspective.

Chaplains who choose the first approach stress that patients have spiritual needs when they enter the hospital. Through screening it is possible to find out what these needs are. It has been empirically proven that patients cope better with their situation when spiritual care is provided. Chaplains look to the medical discipline as an example and try to prove that their work is as professional and as efficient as that of their medical colleagues. The presupposition is that chaplains can play a relevant role during the whole healthcare process.

Not every chaplain chooses this approach. A second group stresses that chaplaincy is not about efficiency at all. Catholic chaplains should avoid imitating other disciplines. What they have to offer is unique. Pastoral care brings the human and the community dimension within the healthcare context. Other disciplines and management should do what they have to do. The task of chaplains, however, is to concentrate on authentic pastoral encounters in which patients and relatives can be themselves.

There is a third response which can be described as interfaith chaplaincy.[13] This approach is not yet well-established, but can be seen as a very promising third way. Catholic chaplains who choose

---

12. Catholic practical theology only started to develop in Belgium as a discipline in the nineties. Not much empirical or qualitative research has been done on healthcare chaplaincy (see for example Dillen et al., "Wat doe jij hier"). The distinction I make here is based on my twenty years of experience as a pastoral supervisor and educator and on my work as editor of the chaplaincy journal *Pastorale Perspectieven*.

13. Van Lierde, "Verschil scherp stellen."

this approach are convinced that they have to look critically at the dominant myths in society and healthcare. They are not social activists who want to change society and institutions from the outside. Rather, they want to change the structure and culture of the hospital from the inside. They realize that they risk minimizing the uniqueness of their identity and practice as Catholic chaplains if they try to imitate other disciplines or professionals. They also realize that within the hospital, when compared to professionals of other faith traditions, they still have a privileged position. However, they do not want to cling to this historical privilege any more. That is why it is not enough for them to concentrate on their counseling and liturgical work. They proactively create room for patients and chaplains who belong to other faith traditions. Interestingly, Catholic chaplains who choose this kind of approach stress that contemplation is a crucial starting point for their work.[14]

The writings and work of Thomas Merton offer us a lens to look closer at the three responses Catholic chaplains give to the changing, high-tech, multi-faith, healthcare landscape in Belgium today.

THOMAS MERTON AS ORGANIZER OF RETREATS

In November 1964 Merton organized an interfaith retreat for peacemakers. Members (lay and clerical) of Catholic, mainline Protestant, historic peace church, and Unitarian traditions participated. It was the time of the Cold War, the Vietnam War, the peace and civil rights movements. The majority of the men (women were not included) who participated were radical pacifists who wanted to change the system from the outside. As such they acted as social activists. Thomas Merton invited them to look with him at "the spiritual roots of protest."[15]

---

14. Ferrant, "Vier Weken."
15. Oyer, *Pursuing Spiritual Roots*. See also Lootens, "Thomas Merton and Spiritual Roots."

Open to the Full Dimension

In December 1967 and May 1968 Merton organized two retreats for contemplative prioresses.[16] He invited them to reflect on their vocation from a prophetic perspective. His aim was not so much to convince them to become social activists. He wanted them to find out what it means to be prophetic as members of established contemplative institutions. Merton organized the two retreats for contemplative prioresses with the substantial support of the Sisters of Loretto.[17] In 1967 Merton made a recording for their Special General Chapter. In the edited version of this recording, one can read how he reflected on the way individuals are pushed to conform to society:

> Now let us remember that there is a whole dialectical relationship between the individual and society and that the individual *has* to be open to others; he has to be responsible and responsive to society; he has to accept the institution as just not a necessary evil, but as a real good in his life. All this we are remembering, but at the same time we also remember the fact that society tends to make things easy for itself by enforcing certain roles upon individuals and making them accept these roles and punishing them for not accepting these roles, and for demanding as a sacrifice of the personality that the person be untrue to himself in order to be true to society. Consequently, whether in secular or religious society, we are constantly finding ourselves in positions where people are rewarded for betraying themselves and betraying those whom they love, and this is praised as an act of sacrifice and homage to the supremacy of the organization.[18]

In Belgium, Catholic chaplains are sent by the diocese. At the same time they are employees of the hospital. This means that they are structurally positioned in a twofold way: within the church and within the healthcare institution. Because of their vocation and double position, Catholic chaplains can experience tensions and

---

16. Thurston, "Absolute Duty to Rebel"; Thurston, "Best Retreat Ever."

17. Kilcourse and Stokell, "Life through the Lens"; Thurston and Swain, *Hidden in the Same Mystery*.

18. Merton, "Comments About Religious Life," 17–18.

ambiguities towards the institutions they work for. I concur with Thurston that within his retreats for contemplative prioresses, Merton offered crucial insights that are "applicable to everyone who is trying to live fully and authentically as a Christian."[19] Merton's insights can support Catholic chaplains in reflecting on their work from a contemplative and prophetic perspective. Furthermore, in doing so they are invited to respond to the healthcare context in Belgium by realizing their vocation as interfaith chaplains.

THOMAS MERTON'S INVITATION TO INTERFAITH CHAPLAINCY

Thomas Merton's writings help to reveal the inadequacy of the first two responses made by Catholic chaplains to the changing healthcare context in Belgium: asserting themselves as real professionals and concentrating exclusively on the unique characteristics of pastoral care. For example, Merton wrote,

> I'll go along with official people as long as I can, but many of the people I'm in tune with—like artists, philosophers, and scientists, are outside the Church. It seems to me that even the progressive voices, Christians among them, are still more or less just Great Society Liberals. They have an optimism that basically accepts the status-quo, and they are not all that different from those who are fearful. They offer some good insights and new images, but for the most part, they're happy, not alienated, and think our society is good and really going somewhere. What they say is useless. In reality, they see no alternative.[20]

A Catholic chaplain who calls herself progressive likes to be related to all kinds of people. In her workplace she wants to build up good relations with management, medical doctors, and professionals in other disciplines. Although she sees herself as related to the church, she stresses the importance of situating herself inside the high-tech, multi-faith, medical institution. She has interesting

19. Thurston, "Best Retreat Ever," 94.
20. Merton, *Springs of Contemplation*, 83–84.

things to say about screening processes, diagnostics, efficiency, and empirical research. Merton subtly makes clear that the risk of her approach is that she becomes a cynic. She accepts that she has to adapt herself to the status quo. For her there is no use in acting prophetically to change the culture and structure of the workplace in order to make it more human and just.

> Some monks feel that it's enough to live a more or less authentic and somewhat updated life. That's not enough, there is no future in that. The mere fact of living an honest life that is also a little bit human may tide us over until we die. There's nothing wrong with it, but in our hearts we know that's not what we're called for. We have to be more than sincere people of prayer.[21]

Merton has a sincere respect for people who try to live an authentic life. A Catholic chaplain who stresses the uniqueness of pastoral care, is an honest person who tries to do just that. She knows that not all the patients call themselves religious. She stresses that chaplaincy is not about proclaiming rules or dogmas, but about personal encounters. However, Merton invites her to dig a little deeper and to look honestly into her heart. She risks feeling secure in her work, without taking into account what is really happening in today's society and healthcare context. He urges her to realize that she could do more than just concentrate on her counseling and liturgical work. Given the inadequacies of the first and second responses, Merton's work then invites the Catholic chaplain to explore the merits of true interfaith chaplaincy.

ACKNOWLEDGING AND EVALUATING THE POWER OF THE CATHOLIC CHAPLAIN

Merton's writing encourages Catholic chaplains to acknowledge and evaluate their own power in relation to patients, other chaplains, and within the healthcare context.

---

21. Merton, *Springs of Contemplation*, 80.

> For centuries the Church has been involved in worldly power. The Church is, in fact, a worldly power. The great problem of contemplative life, of religious life, of the priesthood and of everyone else, is that we have been corrupted by that power. We have been used by this structure to justify a power politics in the Church.[22]

Merton is not afraid to say that he has a privileged position as a Catholic monk, living in the United States. Catholic chaplains who feel marginalized today feel this way exactly because they somehow want to keep the privilege they had until now. Chaplains have to take into account that they have power. Merton invites them to think about what kind of power they have. The question is if using their power to keep their privilege is the most meaningful thing to do. Chaplains have to open their eyes to the fact that they have a responsibility to the people who do not have access to the same kind of power.

ACKNOWLEDGING AND EVALUATING SOCIETY'S SHORTCOMINGS

> We do need praise. It's not good for us to fall on our face, and we have to take that into account. Basically, we have to deal with a mixture of motives, non-Christian motives, ego motives, pagan motives, superstitious motives. There are plenty of these in our racial and ethnic backgrounds. And we carry them with us. But as Christians, we constantly try to rise above these things. Our only real justification is the freedom of the children of God.[23]

Merton invites Catholic chaplains to open themselves to what is going wrong in today's society. There is a one-sided focus on prestige. People need affirmation, of course, but not only based on the position they acquire in society, the amount of money they make, or the technological character of their job. Western society

---

22. Merton, *Springs of Contemplation*, 81.
23. Merton, *Springs of Contemplation*, 103-4.

Open to the Full Dimension

today can be characterized as xenophobic and racist, especially with regard to migrants and refugees with a Muslim background.[24] When we reflect on ourselves, we discover that the characteristics of this society are also in us. In order to open themselves to the world, chaplains are invited to take a critical look at their own mixed motives. That is how they can discover how much they are influenced by the myths which create exclusion and injustice in Western society.

> We have a prophetic task. We have to rock the boat, but not like the hippies. Herbert Marcuse[25] claims that even when you rock the boat you are meeting the demands of a totalitarian society, which requires a certain amount of boat-rockers.[26]

Merton stresses that it is important for social activists to look critically at the work they do. In the end it is possible that their protest actions only strengthen the position of the political and institutional powerbrokers. Catholic chaplains are situated within the structures of the church and the hospital. Based on a contemplative perspective, Merton invites them to become prophets within these contexts.

ACKNOWLEDGING AND SERVING THOSE MOST IN NEED

> We are all sinners. God speaks and we do not listen. On the other hand, the mercy of God is constant. It cannot be overcome. God's promises are absolute. Being Christian doesn't mean "being on the right side." A Christian does not always know where justice lies, does not always see clearly. But the Christian is aware that, while in the human being there is falsity and infidelity, in the mercy of God there is always absolute fidelity. So we reject no

---

24. Fekete, *Suitable Enemy*.
25. Thomas Merton refers here to Marcuse, *One-Dimensional Man*.
26. Merton, *Springs of Contemplation*, 80.

one, but still try to dissociate ourselves from anything that is going to hurt other people. Every Christian has to stand up for the truth that God's mercy is without repentance. God never takes back mercy. We are in a world where many people are in despair. That is where God is really needed. Our Christian witness of mercy is not, after all, credible to a lot of people, because it is not very profound. That is why we have to bear witness to the word of God. The renewal of the whole Church hinges on it. And not just in ideological terms. We also have to dig in and really help those in trouble.[27]

Chaplaincy today developed out of a dialogue between pastoral care and psychotherapy. Because of this, it risks becoming a service that reaches only middle class people. Catholic chaplains have to ask themselves, "Where in the hospital are the people who are most in need?"[28] I remember I did an interview with a chaplain in which she told me that in her work she focuses especially on people who are poor. She gave the example of lobbying for a migrant woman who had just lost her husband and did not have the necessary money to bring him back to his native country for the burial.[29]

ACKNOWLEDGING AND COOPERATING WITH THE RELIGIOUS "OTHER"

> Real charity is involved here. It's a choice between the union of charity with people who are alive and growing and a legalistic union with those who want to hold things back.... This is not something I'm just permitted to do, but something I should do.... If you are choosing for life, for a living entity, it's a better choice. If you are choosing for a dead, rigid thing, it's a worse choice. Even if a choice turns out to be imprudent, there's a built-in

27. Merton, *Springs of Contemplation*, 33–34.
28. Not only chaplains can be concerned about this question. For an intriguing account of nursery care for vulnerable people, based on Thomas Merton, see the article by Fitzgerald et al., "Nurses Need Not Be."
29. Lootens, "Wanneer Men Samen Droomt."

Open to the Full Dimension

safeguard because it's *alive*, it's warm, it's real. We have to choose life, always.[30]

Merton suggests that people who are committed to contemplative living should support life-oriented activities of young people. While studying the life narratives of young Belgian Muslims, I discovered how they are engaged in voluntary work in prisons and hospitals.[31] By doing that, they invite me to support them in their vocation as chaplains. Catholic chaplains can become bridge-builders and introduce them to the hospital. Catholic chaplains can stop clinging to privilege and work proactively in cooperation with Muslims and other marginalized caregivers.

> I'm deeply impregnated with Sufism. In Islam, one of the worst things that any human being can do is to say that there is another besides the One, to act implicitly as if God needed a helper, as if God couldn't do what needs to be done.[32]

Out of his contemplative perspective, Merton developed a keen interest for other faith traditions, in this case Islam. He invites Christians to learn from other traditions. Listening closely to people from other faiths can remind us of our own blind spots. When Catholic chaplains avoid thinking critically about their privileged position within the hospital, they risk behaving like the "saviors" of patients and colleagues of other traditions. Honest discussion can help them to find out how to make their vocation as interfaith chaplains concrete in everyday praxis.

> True unity is the work of love. It is the free union of beings that spontaneously seek to be one in the truth, preserving and elevating their separate selves by self-transcendence. False unity strives to assert itself by the denial of obstacles. True unity admits the presence of

---

30. Merton, *Springs of Contemplation*, 126.
31. Pędziwiatr, *New Muslim Elites*.
32. Merton, *Springs of Contemplation*, 266.

obstacles and of divisions in order to overcome both by humility and sacrifice.[33]

The fragment above comes from a text Thomas Merton wrote in 1962, which is also included in *The Springs of Contemplation*. In this text, he commemorated the shared history of the monks of the Abbey of Gethsemani and the Sisters of Loretto. To support patients and to cooperate with chaplains from other traditions is not always easy. Catholic chaplains are urged not to strive for false unity. Admitting the presence of obstacles and of divisions is an integral part of the process. To see oneself and the other honestly in the eye is also part of it.

CONCLUSION: THE CATHOLIC CHAPLAIN AS PEACEMAKER

During the first retreat, one of the prioresses asked Merton how his view on contemplative living related to his work for peace and non-violence. In his response he made clear that contemplatives can be peacemakers, even when they are positioned within an established institution.

> This is what we have to do: avoid lining up on the side of a revolution as well as on the side of a counter-revolution. We need to line up on the side of the people. Wherever there is human presence, we have to be present to it. And wherever there is a person, there has to be personal communication. There Christ can work. Where there is presence, there is God. A Christian is one who continues to communicate across all the boundaries, a sign of hope for a convergence back to a kind of unity.[34]

Catholic chaplains can learn from Merton that it is important and meaningful to stress the uniqueness of pastoral care: it is about presence and personal communication. But this is not enough. Looking from a contemplative and prophetic perspective,

---

33. Merton, *Springs of Contemplation*, 284.
34. Merton, *Springs of Contemplation*, 31.

it is also necessary to communicate across boundaries. As such chaplains can offer pastoral care for migrants with a different religious background.

One of the dominant boundaries in today's European society is the "clash of civilizations" myth in which migrants with a Muslim background are seen as essentially different from White people. Based on a contemplative and prophetic perspective, Merton invites Catholic chaplains to question their privileged position. He urges them to look at today's context and he invites them to involve themselves in the introduction of and the cooperation with chaplains of other faith traditions, especially Islam. As such they can become peacemakers within a high-tech hospital and realize their vocation as interfaith chaplains.

2

Thomas Merton, Migration, and Practical Theology

Never believe that I am some different being from you because I am here in a very quiet monastery without problems like yours. Much to the contrary, I live in the heart of your problem because I live in the heart of the Church. I do not believe myself truly a monk, or truly a priest, if I were not able to feel in myself all of the revolts and all of the anguish of modern man.[1]

There is a mental ecology, too, a living balance of spirits in this corner of the woods. There is room here for many other songs beside those of birds. Of Vallejo, for instance. . . . Or the dry disconcerting voice of Nicanor Parra . . . Chuang Tzu . . . a Syrian hermit called Philoxenus. . . . Here is heard the clanging prose of Tertullian, with the dry catarrh of Sartre. Here the voluble dissonances of Auden, with the golden sounds of John of Salisbury. Here is the deep vegetation of that more ancient forest in which the angry birds, Isaias and Jeremias, sing. Here

1. Merton and Ocampo, *Fragmentos de un Regalo*, 70–71.

Open to the Full Dimension

should be, and are, feminine voices from Angela of Foligno to Flannery O'Connor, Theresa of Avila, Juliana of Norwich, and, more personally and warmly still, Raissa Maritain. It is good to choose the voices that will be heard in these woods, but they also choose themselves, and send themselves here to be present in this silence.[2]

IN 2012, THE BRITISH theologian Susanna Snyder published *Asylum-Seeking, Migration and Church*. With this practical-theological book, Snyder wants to "provide sustenance and motivation for Christians supporting migrants, inspire and encourage others to become involved and hint at directions for ongoing work."[3] She defines her approach as a Performative and Liberatory Theology.[4] In her book, she brings forced migration studies and biblical studies in dialogue with each other. In the first chapter of part 3, she gives a general overview of the approach to strangers in the Bible: in the New Testament, Christians see themselves as people "on the move." To actualize this idea, she quotes Thomas Merton,[5] who, in one of his most known prayers, describes himself as someone on the road:

> My Lord God, l have no idea where l am going. I do not see the road ahead of me. I cannot know for certain where it will end. Nor do I really know myself, and the fact that I think that I am following your will does not mean that I am actually doing so. But I believe that the desire to please you does in fact please you. And I hope I have that desire in all that I am doing. I hope that I will never do anything apart from that desire. And I know that if I do this you will lead me by the right road though I may know nothing about it. Therefore will I trust you always though I may seem to be lost and in the shadow

---

2. Merton, *Day of a Stranger*, 35–37.
3. Snyder, *Asylum-Seeking*, 210.
4. Snyder, *Asylum-Seeking*, 15–34.
5. Merton, *Thoughts in Solitude*, 83.

of death. I will not fear, for you are ever with me, and you will never leave me to face my perils alone.[6]

Snyder stresses that it is important for her as a researcher that she practices critical self-reflection and that her theological approach invites further exploration: "These perspectives, along with the research methodology and findings should be critiqued by others and the researcher needs to be willing to change her mind and presuppositions as a result."[7] She quotes Emmanuel Y. Lartey,[8] who advocates an intercultural practical theology which is "polylingual, polyphonic, and polyperspectival. Many voices need to be spoken, listened to and respected in our quest for meaningful and effective living."[9]

As a practical theologian, one of the voices I listen to regularly is Thomas Merton. I have read Snyder's book with his voice in the back of my mind. In this review, I want to bring the perspectives of Snyder into dialogue with Merton. I agree with Pearson who states: "The escalating extremism in numerous countries, the rise of the far right, and the all-too-frequent scapegoating of immigrants and other groups would, I feel certain, be a subject of Merton's pen were he writing today."[10]

I see this review as a hermeneutical exercise in which the perspectives of Merton and Snyder enrich each other. Merton wrote in the forties, fifties, and sixties of the twentieth century. Today's global context is somehow different. This means that what he wrote then, cannot be naively understood today. I am inspired by the hermeneutical method developed by the historical theologian Margaret Miles. She has based her approach on Martha Nussbaum. Miles calls her hermeneutical method "Reading for life."[11]

---

6. Quoted partly in Snyder, *Asylum-Seeking*, 136.
7. Snyder, *Asylum-Seeking*, 20.
8. Lartey, *Pastoral Theology*, 124.
9. Quoted in Snyder, *Asylum-Seeking*, 21.
10. Pearson, "Voice for Racial Justice," 47.
11. Miles, *Reading for Life*.

Reading for life is different than reading for entertainment. It is also different than reading to understand the author's communication. It is not academic reading, assigned reading. Reading for life desperately seeks suggestions—clues—about how to get what I most deeply long for.[12]

A MONK AT THE MARGIN AND A RESEARCHER AS INSIDER-OUTSIDER

In 1968, Thomas Merton gave an informal talk in Calcutta in which he described himself as a person at the margin:

> The monk in the modern world is no longer an established person with an established place in society. We realize very keenly in America today that the monk is essentially outside of all establishments. He does not belong to an establishment. He is a marginal person who withdraws deliberately to the margin of society with a view to deepening fundamental human experience.[13]

Situating himself at the margin, he accepts his social-historical position within American society.[14] Seeing himself as part of the Catholic Church he is aware of his complicity in worldly power:

> For centuries the Church has been involved in worldly power. The Church is, in fact, a worldly power. The great problem of contemplative life, of religious life, of the priesthood and of everyone else, is that we have been corrupted by that power. We have been used by this structure to justify a power politics in the Church.[15]

---

12. Miles, *Recollections*, 76.
13. Merton, *Asian Journal*, 305.
14. Bielawski, "Merton's Margin," 81–83.
15. Merton, *Springs of Contemplation*, 81.

According to Mark Meade, Merton is convinced that he also must implicate himself in the violence of the world and recognize that to be aware of these evils is to be a "guilty bystander."[16]

Susanna Snyder describes herself as "a white, 33-year-old, British, middle-class, ordained Anglican woman."[17] As a researcher, she sees herself as an insider-outsider: "I, as a British citizen, sometimes refer to established communities in the UK using the pronoun 'we', and newly-arrived migrants as 'they.' I refer to Christian groups and churches variously as 'they' and 'we' in recognition of the fact that I was an outsider to most of the organizations, but also an insider through being a Christian involved in volunteer work."[18]

She asks herself how she can listen in a responsible way to people seeking sanctuary: "Practicing reflexivity helps to maintain an awareness of power differentials between the story-teller and listener."[19] In encountering the powers, Christians who are members of established communities "must own the part their forebears and tradition have played in creating a number of the underlying push factors that cause refugees to flee today and the fiercely defended state borders that they encounter."[20]

GOING BEYOND DEATH AND INHABITING AN ECOLOGY OF FAITH

In the informal talk he gave in Calcutta, Merton describes the existential dimension of being at the margin. He identified himself with the displaced person and the prisoner:

> The marginal person, the monk, the displaced person, the prisoner, all these people live in the presence of death, which calls into question the meaning of life. He struggles with the fact of death in himself, trying

16. Meade, "From Downtown Louisville," 176.
17. Snyder, *Asylum-Seeking*, 20.
18. Snyder, *Asylum-Seeking*, 12.
19. Snyder, *Asylum-Seeking*, 25.
20. Snyder, *Asylum-Seeking*, 206.

Open to the Full Dimension

to seek something deeper than death; because there is something deeper than death, and the office of the monk or the marginal person, the meditative person or the poet is to go beyond death even in this life, to go beyond the dichotomy of life and death and to be, therefore, a witness to life.[21]

Snyder talks about displaced persons when she explains the term "forced migrants." It refers "to those who have fled their homes involuntarily, whether within their own country or to another state. It includes refugees, internally displaced persons (IDPs), post-conflict returnees, and environmental and development displacees."[22]

In the first chapter of part 3 of her book, Snyder analyzes the Greek word *paroikos*, which is used in the first letter of Peter.[23] She quotes Elliot who translates this term as "foreign" or "other." It refers to a "displaced and dislocated person, the curious or suspicious-looking alien or stranger."[24]

During their journey to the global north, and after their arrival, forced migrants are confronted with the risk of death: "social, psychological, personal, or even physical."[25] Members of established communities in the north can avoid looking death in the eye. When they do so, they risk transforming their fear of death "into something tangible by locating it in agents who are different from us and have the power to kill us."[26] As such, migrants are experienced as an existential threat.

Snyder analyzes the biblical stories of Ruth and the Syrophoenician woman because as insiders-outsiders they inhabit an "ecology of faith." Snyder quotes Phyllis Trible who argues that Ruth was able to make a commitment beyond death: "A young woman has committed herself to the life of an old woman rather than to

---

21. Merton, *Asian Journal*, 306.
22. Snyder, *Asylum-Seeking*, 10.
23. Snyder, *Asylum-Seeking*, 134.
24. Elliot, *Home for the Homeless*, 23–25.
25. Pattison, *Shame*, 183.
26. Snyder, *Asylum-Seeking*, 101.

the search of a husband, and she has made this commitment not 'until death do us part' but beyond death . . . there is no more radical decision in all the memories of Israel."[27]

Snyder states that it is the responsibility of local churches to help change the attitudes of church members who belong to established communities and who experience asylum seekers as an existential threat. This cannot be done when their fear is not taken seriously. The richness of the stories of Ruth and the Syrophoenician woman is that they are present as fully fleshed characters. According to Snyder, they have their strengths but also their flaws. They are privileged and marginalized at the same time. They have mixed motives. That is why these women can be an inspiration both for members of established communities and for people seeking sanctuary.

Merton similarly believes that we all have mixed motives. Living as a Christian means accepting the existence of these motives and moving beyond them. The monk, the meditative person or the poet does this by struggling with the fact of death in himself.

> Basically, we have to deal with a mixture of motives, non-Christian motives, ego motives, pagan motives, superstitious motives. There are plenty of these in our racial and ethnic backgrounds. And we carry them with us. But as Christians, we constantly try to rise above these things. Our only real justification is the freedom of the children of God.[28]

THE GREAT DOUBT AND COURAGEOUS BOUNDARY-CROSSING

Being a monk implies accepting doubt. During his talk in Calcutta, Merton also described the religious process that is related to being a person at the margin:

> As soon as you say faith in terms of this monastic and marginal existence you run into another problem. Faith

27. Trible, *God and Rhetoric*, 173.
28. Merton, *Springs of Contemplation*, 103–4.

Open to the Full Dimension

means doubt. Faith is not the suppression of doubt. It is the overcoming of doubt, and you overcome doubt by going through it. The man of faith who has never experienced doubt is not a man of faith. Consequently, the monk is one who has to struggle within the debts of his being with the presence of doubt and to go through what some religions call the Great Doubt, to break through beyond doubt into a [certitude] which is very, very deep, because it is not his own personal [certitude], it is the [certitude] of God Himself, in us. The only ultimate reality is God. God lives and dwells in us.[29]

At the beginning of chapter 1, Snyder shares with the reader her personal motivation to write her book:

> I had long been interested in issues of justice and development and their relationship to Christian faith, and had, for instance, visited Mozambique in 2003 when it was still recovering from civil war in which four million people had been displaced. I was also feeling in "exile" myself. I was passing through theological college and at an in-between stage personally, struggling with my faith, aspects of the institutional church and a sense of not belonging in a diverse theological training environment. A personal sense of being out of place, I am sure, drew me to others who were far more literally and profoundly displaced.[30]

As a monk, Merton wanted to live an honest religious life. He was courageously able to cross cultural and religious boundaries. Through his correspondence he engaged "in rigorous conversation with thinkers from all faiths and intellectual backgrounds—atheists, poets, novelists, feminists, Muslims, Protestants, Byzantine Orthodox and communists."[31] One of the people he was in conversation with was the Pakistan Sufi Abdul Aziz. Aziz was looking for someone to talk with about Christian mysticism. It was Louis Massignon, the French peace-activist and a mutual friend, who suggested to Aziz to

29. Merton, *Asian Journal*, 306.
30. Snyder, *Asylum-Seeking*, 6.
31. Inchausti, *Thinking through Thomas Merton*, 132.

write to Merton.[32] Although they never met face to face, these two religious men were able to talk with each other in a very honest and empathic way. In one of his letters, Aziz asked Merton to share with him the way he prayed. This is what Merton answered:

> Strictly speaking I have a very simple way of prayer. It is centered entirely on attention to the presence of God and to His will and His love. That is to say that it is centered on *faith* by which alone we can know the presence of God. One might say this gives my meditation the character described by the Prophet as "being before God as if you saw Him." Yet it does not mean imagining anything or conceiving a precise image of God, for to my mind this would be a kind of idolatry. On the contrary, it is a matter of adoring Him as invisible and infinitely beyond our comprehension, and realizing Him as all. My prayer tends very much toward what you call *fana*. There is in my heart this great thirst to recognize totally the nothingness of all that is not God. My prayer is then a kind of praise rising up out of the center of Nothing and Silence. If I am still present "myself" this I recognize as an obstacle about which I can do nothing unless He Himself removes the obstacle. If He wills He can then make the Nothingness into a total clarity.[33]

One of the ways people from established communities can inhabit an "ecology of faith" is by courageous boundary-crossing. Snyder describes the word "ecology" as "a way of living and being which is trusting and compassionate towards those who are unknown. 'Faith' is used to indicate the opposite of fear rather than a system of religious doctrines and practices."[34]

Engaging in honest dialogue with people seeking sanctuary can be spiritually transforming for the person who listens attentively. People seeking sanctuary point us towards a realization that "God is that which cannot be fully grasped by our language and

---

32. Thurston, "Islam in Alaska," 3.
33. Merton, *Hidden Ground of Love*, 63–64.
34. Snyder, *Asylum-Seeking*, 163.

Open to the Full Dimension

bound by our experiences and fantasies. God always exists outside any totalitarian effort and resists any attempt of full narration."[35]

ORGANIZING RETREATS AND ENCOUNTERING WITH THE POWERS

Snyder asks herself how established church communities can be prophetic in a society that is dominated by an "ecology of fear." In the last part of her book, she offers "a vision of a more faithful ecology within which renewed praxis could take place and a few general but realistic suggestions for practice within this ecology."[36] She clusters these suggestions within a fourfold typology: encounters of grassroots service, encounters with the powers, encounters in worship, and encounters in theology.

In December 1967 and May 1968, Merton organized two retreats for contemplative prioresses. He invited the participants to reflect on their vocation from a prophetic perspective. He wanted them to find out what it meant to be prophetic as members of established contemplative communities. During one of these retreats, Merton discusses the relation between theology, worship, and grassroots service. He says:

> We are in a world where many people are in despair. That's where God is really needed. Our Christian witness of mercy is not, after all, credible to a lot of people, because it is not very profound. That is why we have to bear witness to the word of God. The renewal of the whole Church hinges on it. And not just in ideological terms. We also have to dig in and really help those in trouble.[37]

Merton stresses that within a troubled world, theology and worship can only be done in an honest way when they are related to grassroots service. Snyder shares the same concern regarding

---

35. Kwok, "Theology of Border Passage," 114.
36. Snyder, *Asylum-Seeking*, 32.
37. Merton, *Springs of Contemplation*, 34.

theology when she quotes Peter C. Phan.[38] This theologian invites his colleagues to "dig deep into the humus of the immigrants' lives."[39]

Merton learned a lot by listening carefully to his Muslim friend, Abdul Aziz. He also read a lot about Sufism and taught his novices about it. Based on this learning process he warns the members of contemplative communities that there is a pitfall in helping people in need:

> I'm deeply impregnated with Sufism. In Islam, one of the worst things that any human being can do is to say that there is an other besides the One, to act implicitly as if God needed a helper, as if God couldn't do what needs to be done.[40]

Snyder, too, is keenly aware of the danger of acting in a paternalistic or exploitative way: "Mutuality needs to lie at the heart of all encounters between migrants and supporters, and Christians must go beyond an approach that is only about duty towards one that is also about reciprocally enriching relationship and flourishing."[41]

Through his friendship with peace-activists,[42] his study of authors like Herbert Marcuse, and his own contemplative activism, Merton was well informed about the complexity of acting prophetically through engaging the powers:

> We have a prophetic task. We have to rock the boat, but not like the hippies. Herbert Marcuse claims that even when you rock the boat you are meeting the demands of a totalitarian society, which requires a certain amount of boat-rockers.[43]

Snyder calls grassroots service the "cuddlesome" face of religion. While talking about advocacy and lobbying, she ironically argues that activities "that encounter the powers represent 'admirably

---

38. Snyder, *Asylum-Seeking*, 24.
39. Phan, "Experience of Migration," 161.
40. Merton, *Springs of Contemplation*, 266.
41. Snyder, *Asylum-Seeking*, 198.
42. Lootens, "Thomas Merton and Spiritual Roots."
43. Merton, *Springs of Contemplation*, 80.

troublesome' religion."[44] Although encountering the powers can be effective, members of established church communities cannot easily predict what the result of their prophetic actions will be.

CONCLUSION

Snyder has written an eloquent book in which she succeeds in developing "a more realistic theology."[45] In bringing about new perspectives for pastoral care with migrants, she has taken seriously an "ecology of fear" which is metaphorically and materially present in established communities in the United Kingdom today. At the same time, she tentatively shows us "gradual steps" towards an "ecology of faith."[46]

> We believe that our future will be made by love and hope, not by violence or calculation. The Spirit of Life that has brought us together, whether in space or only in agreement, will make our encounter an epiphany of certainties we could not know in isolation.[47]

During his lifetime, Merton succeeded in creating "a *spiritual* community which transcends national, social and especially tribal limitations."[48] Being a European born in France who came to the United States after studying in the United Kingdom, he was an insider-outsider of the society in which he lived. Like many migrants today, he was a living example of "transnationalism." As a monk, master of novices, organizer of retreats, and letter writer he lived socio-historically, existentially, and spiritually at the margin with an impressive openness to the violence and anguish people experienced around the world. The contemplative and activist life that he shared with other contemplatives and peace-activists of other traditions and denominations made him at the same time, humble and hopeful. As such he inhabited an "ecology of faith."

44. Snyder, *Asylum-Seeking*, 40.
45. Snyder, *Asylum-Seeking*, 147.
46. Snyder, *Asylum-Seeking*, 33.
47. Merton, *Literary Essays*, 371.
48. Merton, *Search for Solitude*, 341.

3

Thomas Merton and Pastoral Supervision

Avoid three kinds of masters:
Those who esteem only themselves,
For their self-esteem is blindness;
Those who esteem only innovations,
For their opinions are aimless,
Without meaning;
Those who esteem only what is established;
Their minds
Are little cells of ice.[1]

I HAVE BEEN ACTIVE as a pastoral supervisor in Flanders since 2002. In 2012, I became co-conductor of the Professional Accompaniment course at the Center for Christian Education in Antwerp. In 2016, I became coordinator of a new Pastoral Supervision

---

1. Merton, *Raids on the Unspeakable*, 148.

Open to the Full Dimension

course, organized by Caritas Flanders and the Flemish Center for Christian Education. Over the years, I have studied a variety of reference works. They helped me to broaden and deepen my own vision on pastoral supervision. One of the authors who particularly inspired me in this respect was Thomas Merton.

Prior to the new Pastoral Supervision course, my two colleagues, Sybryn Leirs and Johan Hovelynck, along with myself, went looking for a handbook that matched our vision. As if by chance, we came across the book by Jane Leach and Michael Paterson.[2] Since then, it has been an important guide in our training. It is therefore a good thing that this book is also available in Dutch.[3]

As I went through the book, my conviction grew that the vision of Leach and Paterson could be strengthened, broadened, and deepened by bringing them into dialogue with the work of Thomas Merton. To illustrate, in this chapter I will discuss fragments from some of his writings. Merton can help me look at pastoral supervision from a contemplative and prophetic perspective. Leach and Paterson provide me with inspiration to reflect on my work from a theological and prophetic perspective. Merton also invites me to place my commitment as a supervisor within an eschatological perspective.

In the first section, I will briefly consider whether Thomas Merton can be a conversation partner as I think about the identity of pastoral supervision from a contemplative and prophetic perspective. I will look at the similarities and differences between Merton on one hand, and Leach and Paterson on the other.

In the second section, I bring the APSE[4] definition of pastoral supervision into conversation with Merton's work. This definition was co-developed by Leach and Paterson and plays a fundamental role throughout their book.

The following two sections are devoted to two basic ideas of Leach and Paterson. They describe pastoral supervision as

---

2. Leach and Paterson, *Pastoral Supervision*.
3. Leach and Paterson, with Lootens, *Pastorale Supervisie*.
4. APSE: Association of Pastoral Supervisors and Educators (UK).

attention and transformation. These are two concepts that also play an important role in Merton's work.

In the last section, I will consider the existential and practical consequences that Merton attaches to the concept of eschatology. On this basis, pastoral supervision can be described as a form of nonviolent action.

THOMAS MERTON AS CONVERSATION PARTNER

For Merton, it is important to develop a Christian perspective on contemplation that is relevant for the world in which we live. Contemplation is not indifferent to history and time. Contemplation and active living are strongly related to each other. Because of this characteristic, Christian contemplation can be meaningfully discussed with people who belong to other faith traditions.

> Very often, in describing contemplative experience, especially when attempting to do so in a way that will embrace both "Christian" and "Oriental" contemplation, writers tend to do it in a way that arises other serious difficulties. For instance, they will emphasize the element of psycho logical introversion, or withdrawal from sensible reality, of intense recollection and inner unity, of sublime peace, of spiritual joy above and beyond all sensible satisfaction, and so on. There is certainly a basis for such descriptions, but are they not in the end completely misleading? Do they not represent a caricature of contemplation rather than its authentic description? Do they not assert that contemplation is exclusively negative and world-denying, and declare that contemplative life is one which is totally indifferent to the world, to history, and to time? And in that case, can one avoid the conclusion that contemplation, whether Eastern or Western, is equally useless, selfish, passive, barren, and therefore inadmissible?[5]

Leach and Paterson write in their Preface that they want to offer an alternative for those who do not find themselves in the

---

5. Merton, *Mystics & Zen Masters*, 210–211.

Open to the Full Dimension

therapeutic paradigms that are dominant in the existing supervision literature. In their book, they do not explicitly view pastoral supervision from a contemplative perspective. The term "contemplative" is only mentioned when the developmental stages of supervisors are discussed in chapter 5. Stage 4 is described by them as "contemplation in action as supervisees sense the action of God in their work, see gospel stories unfold before them and make connections between theology and life."[6] They situate contemplation within the process of theological reflection.

Leach and Paterson come close to Merton's view on contemplation when they refer to two well-known contemporary spiritual authors: Rowan Williams and Parker J. Palmer. Rowan Williams is strongly moved by Thomas Merton's thinking. He dedicated a book to him in 2013.[7] Parker J. Palmer is an author who regularly refers to the writings of Thomas Merton.[8]

> Instead of building our ideas of contemplation upon a few superficial modern manuals which, themselves, take only a foreshortened perspective of the Christian mystical tradition, let us remind ourselves of the full, liturgical, biblical and patristic dimensions of Christian mysticism.[9]

As a contemplative monk, Thomas Merton was very familiar with liturgy, the Bible, and patristic authors. On this basis, he succeeded to describe the identity of contemplation in the Christian tradition. For Leach and Paterson, liturgy and Bible reading can be a starting point for theological reflection.[10] Talking about the supervision process, they describe the use of rituals, prayer, and Bible reading as allowing God to host and contain the supervisor and supervisee.[11]

---

6. Leach and Paterson, *Pastoral Supervision*, 133.
7. Williams, *Silent Action*.
8. Palmer, *Active Life*; Palmer, *Promise of Paradox*.
9. Merton, *Mystics & Zen Masters*, 212.
10. Leach and Paterson, *Pastoral Supervision*, 81.
11. Leach and Paterson, *Pastoral Supervision*, 45

Thomas Merton and Pastoral Supervision

For Merton, the authenticity of the Christian contemplative experience becomes clear when it goes hand in hand with a basic prophetic attitude. He reflects on contemplation from an ecumenical and interreligious perspective. For him, the concept of "Church" has primarily a theological meaning and is not used by him merely to refer to the Roman Catholic Church.

> Christian contemplation must be able to show the Asian contemplative . . . that he is not confined to the fussy and materialistic individualism of purely ethical and practical concerns. That he is, above all, dissociated from the crudeness and brutality of a society that seeks to thrive on purely material and scientific exploration. It must also show modern man that Christianity is deeply aware of the power at work in history while at the same time defending him against the demonic illusion that comes from identifying the Church with the interests of this or that side in the inhuman struggle for political power.[12]

Leach and Paterson look for the uniqueness of pastoral supervision from an ecumenical and intercultural perspective. They also use the word "Church" as a theological concept, and not as a description of a particular denomination. In that case, they use the word "church" in lowercase. Leach and Paterson stress that pastoral supervision can have a prophetic dimension. At the end of chapter 10, they describe pastoral supervision as a "prophetic ministry of real presence."[13]

Thomas Merton hasn't written a manual on pastoral supervision. He has regularly thought about the specificity of spiritual direction. Merton did this by looking at what can be found in the desert mothers and fathers.[14] He noticed that people who lived and worked in the city as well as disciples, went to visit these experienced teachers.[15] On the basis of this observation he came to his description of spiritual direction.

12. Merton, *Mystics & Zen Masters*, 213–14.
13. Leach and Paterson, *Pastoral Supervision*, 255.
14. Merton, *Wisdom of the Desert*; Merton, *Contemplation in a World*.
15. The spiritual scholar Sheldrake argues that Merton had a strong affinity

Open to the Full Dimension

This brings us to the root meaning of spiritual direction. It is a continuous process of formation and guidance, in which a Christian is led and encouraged *in his special vocation*, so that by faithful correspondence to the graces of the Holy Spirit he may attend to the particular end of his vocation and to union with God.[16]

He is convinced that both in active life and in monastic life, it is important to experience unity with God and other people. Because of the connection he makes with the desert mothers and fathers, he is an interesting conversation partner given the singularity of pastoral supervision.

Besides *renewal* of our own tradition we must of course obviously *adapt* ourselves to the needs of our time, and a return to tradition does not mean trying to revive, in all its details, the life lived by the early monks, or trying to do all the things that they did. But it means living in our time and solving the problems of our time in the way and with the spirit in which they lived in a different time and solved different problems.[17]

As a novice master and spiritual director at the abbey, Merton was interested in the renewal of the monastic life. As such, he was working in a different context and time. As a letter writer and organizer of retreats, Merton was exercising what he called a ministry of friendship.[18] He was keenly interested in the lives and professional tasks of the many people with whom he was in contact.

---

with the desert mothers and fathers. These desert ascetics took on different social roles: "the holy men and women of the early Christian centuries did not leave social or public roles behind entirely. Especially in Syria, ascetics continued to live close to human habitation and remained visible challenges near where people lived. . . . In general, by standing socially and geographically on the margins, the early ascetics were often accepted as spiritual guides and even at times took on the roles of local leadership or of social arbitrator. In a sense, Merton seems to be offering a reinterpretation of this ancient role." Sheldrake, *Explorations in Spirituality*, 136.

16. Merton, *Spiritual Direction & Meditation*, 13.
17. Merton, *Cassian and the Fathers*, 6.
18. Merton, *Life in Letters*, xi–xii.

Merton invites me to find the spirit in which he was working as a spiritual director and pastoral practitioner. He did this himself by reading and reflecting on the lives and texts of the desert mothers and fathers. At the same time, I have to situate my task as pastoral supervisor within my own context and time.

PASTORAL SUPERVISION IS . . .

A Regular, Planned, Intentional and Boundaried Space

> What people seek today is not so much the organized, predigested routine of conferences and exercises, but an opportunity to be quiet, to reflect, and to discuss in informational, spontaneous and friendly encounters the things they have on their minds.[19]

As a monk, Merton was familiar with attending conferences and practicing Christian meditation. He saw the value but also the limitations of it. As a spiritual director and pastoral practitioner, Merton was looking for what drives people in society. One of the things that struck him was that everyone takes on all kinds of social roles, but often they do not have their own mature identity. That's why he saw the need to create places of dialogue where people could think about the different roles in an interactive way.

Pastoral supervision is intended to be a place where a supervisor and supervisees engage in a dialogue about professional experiences. At the end of chapter 1, Leach and Paterson refer to the "three-legged chair of supervision."[20] Pastoral supervision has a restorative, formative, and normative function. The aim is, among other things, to pronounce forgotten or overlooked aspects of oneself, to grow in the professional assignment, and, in an informed manner, reflect on the supervision approach as it relates to the context in which one is professionally active. Ultimately,

---

19. Merton, *Contemplation in a World*, 139.
20. Leach and Paterson, *Pastoral Supervision*, 21.

Open to the Full Dimension

pastoral supervision is a place of dialogue where one can discover one's own unique professional identity and allow it to develop.

A Relationship

In the Sayings of the desert mothers and fathers, the spiritual director is called a Master. The person who is learning how to live as a hermit, is called a disciple.

> At this point, passing from the viewpoint of the disciple to that of the Master, we see that the Master must be extraordinarily humble, discerning, kind, and in no sense a despotic character. The "hard sayings" which he administers must spring from genuine kindness and concern for the interests of the disciples and not from a secret desire to dominate and exploit them for his own egotistic ends. The Master must, in other words, be himself one who is no longer in the least attracted by "superiority" or by the desire to rule and teach others.[21]

Merton discovered that the desert mothers and fathers were often reluctant to become teachers. It was a spiritual learning process for them to discover that this task was part of their vocation as a hermit. The people came to see them because they saw how these teachers, themselves, had gone through a process of honest self-examination.

Throughout the book, Leach and Paterson regularly indicate how important it is for pastoral supervisors to receive supervision. This is necessary in order to refine one's own craft in a safe and confidential context and honestly face one's own motives.

Spiritually Rich

> It is of course quite true that the contemplative life can be lived outside a monastery, and that one can be closely united to God while leading a life of considerable activity.

---

21. Merton, *Contemplation in a World*, 289.

> Nevertheless, a certain dimension of inner solitude and peace is necessary for this intimate union with God. However, we must always remember that union with God is not a matter of withdrawal and of special experiences, so much as it is a question of love, and the love of other men is necessary if we are to grow without illusions in the authentic love of God. The two loves are in fact one, and they are in no sense obstacles to each other.[22]

Thomas Merton gives a Christian interpretation to the word, "contemplation." He is rather skeptical about a generic interpretation of this concept. This is because contemplation risks being reduced to a form of narcissism. In Christian contemplation, your socially constructed identity is fundamentally questioned. This is not an easy process, in fact you are never done with it in practice.

In chapter 3, Leach and Paterson show how pastoral supervision can be understood as a process of spiritual growth, in which the supervisor learns to listen to the voices of people on the margins,—those who are socially invisible and are not heard. From a spiritual perspective, the pastoral supervisor can experience how the supervisee uniquely relates to God and other people.

Theologically Rich

> Without experienced guides who are completely open to the full dimension—the mystical and prophetic dimension—of love in Christ, renewal will mean little more than the replacement of old rules by new ones and of old traditions by novel frenzies.[23]

As a monk and novice master, Merton gave a contemplative interpretation to the concept of theology. There is a need for scientific theological reflection, but this should not be detached from one's own spiritual growth. In his reflection, Merton strongly based himself on the Bible and the desert mothers and fathers. He was

---

22. Merton, *Contemplation in a World*, 234.
23. Merton, *Contemplation in a World*, 25.

convinced that this would provide the material for a theology that understands the importance of a profound renewal of church and society. At the beginning of each chapter, Leach and Paterson invite the reader to reflect on a specific aspect of pastoral supervision on the basis of a Biblical fragment. They describe pastoral supervision in chapter 1 as a "covenant relationship."[24] They reflect on this theologically from the point of view of Trinity. This perspective helps supervisees think about their professional identity. The Trinity forms a theological foundation for the prophetic interpretation that Leach and Paterson give to pastoral supervision.

Psychologically Informed

> I suppose we could say that in a certain way we are all slightly nuts. We are all a little bit crazy and we all have to get along with one another in spite of our little eccentricities and quirks of character. There is evidently a little bit of the neurotic in almost everybody today. This has to be understood and accepted. Anyway the great thing is to maintain a healthy atmosphere.[25]

For Thomas Merton, the psychological dimension cannot be ignored. Psychological reflection can help to better understand certain personal and relational difficulties. However, psychology should not be used to put a person in a box. After all, this makes it too easy for the spiritual director to stay out of harm's way. The use of psychological insights is useful when it allows you to strengthen the relationship you have with the other person.

Leach and Paterson are convinced that it is good to make use of psychological insights. In chapter 4 they examine the relevance of the "drama triangle" for pastoral supervision.[26] For them, it's not about getting a psychological diagnosis from the supervisor. They place the use of psychological insights within a relational perspective.

---

24. Leach and Paterson, *Pastoral Supervision*, 17–19.
25. Merton, *Contemplation in a World*, 377.
26. Leach and Paterson, *Pastoral Supervision*, 97–106.

Contextually Sensitive

> Nowadays when we talk so much of freedom, commitment, "engagement" and so on, it becomes imperative to ask whether the choices we are making have any meaning whatever. Do they change anything? Do they get us anywhere? Do we really choose to alter the direction of our lives or do we simply comfort ourselves with the choice of making another choice? Can we really decide effectively for a better world?[27]

No matter where you are, Merton believes that you cannot pretend that the social context does not exist. If one does so, one inevitably identifies with the dominant groups in society. At the same time, he realizes that it is not easy to make effective social change. He, himself, chooses to enter into a friendly dialogue with writers, poets, young people, religious people, nonbelievers, and social activists, in order to identify as much as possible with people who are on the margins of society.

Leach and Paterson emphasize seeing pastoral supervision as a specific context. It is important for the supervisor to deal with this context in a responsible and transparent manner. At the same time, the supervisor and the supervisee are also in a broader context. It is possible that they meet professionally outside the context of supervision, and because of the supervision process, it is important to explicitly consider this.

Leach and Paterson deal with the social context when they focus on the theme of diversity, in terms of gender, sexual orientation, disability, age, social background, ethnicity, and religious beliefs. In chapter 8 they show how important it is to think about one's own social identity as a supervisor since this is linked to different forms of power.

---

27. Merton, *Contemplation in a World*, 150.

Open to the Full Dimension

Praxis-based

> To choose the world is not then merely a pious admission that the world is acceptable because it comes from the hand of God. It is first of all an acceptance of a task and a vocation in the world, in history and in time, which is the present. To choose the world is to choose to do the work I am capable of doing, in collaboration with my brother, to make the world better, more free, more just, more livable, more human.[28]

Thomas Merton spent his entire life looking for ways to give concrete form to his identity as a monk. He discovered that he could do this best, not by isolating himself from the world, but by working together with other people and engaging in dialogue. He became more and more convinced that monastic life is aimed at a deep connection and solidarity with the world outside the abbey.

Leach has developed an intercultural method for theological reflection which is strongly praxis-based.[29] This method has its roots in feminist theology and liberation theology. It plays a central role in the book on pastoral supervision that she wrote with Paterson. She poses five questions that can be helpful for pastoral practitioners to reflect on theologically, when it comes to concrete professional experiences whether in a group or individually.

1. Whose voices can you hear (and whose are silent)?
2. What are the wider issues implicit here?
3. What are your own hearts saying?
4. What does the Christian tradition have to say?
5. What, in the light of all this, is the mission of the church, and within that, your task, here and now?

It is an approach that encourages supervisees to make their theological presuppositions explicit and investigate the extent to

---

28. Merton, *Contemplation in a World*, 149.
29. Leach, "Pastoral Theology as Attention."

A Way of Growing In

In his writings, Thomas Merton distinguishes between the false self and the true self. The false self coincides with the roles we take on in society, those that give us the necessary confirmation. This can give one the feeling of belonging. There's nothing wrong with that. However, from a contemplative and prophetic perspective, Merton poses the question of whether we can be satisfied with this. The true self coincides with the identity given to us by God as a gift. As long as we identify with our social roles in a one-sided way, we cannot discover this true self. Letting go of the false self is a difficult and lifelong process.

> Our vocation is not simply to *be*, but to work together with God in the creation of our own life, our own identity, our own destiny. We are free beings and sons of God. This means to say that we should not passively exist, but actively participate in His creative freedom, in our own lives, and in the lives of others, by choosing the truth. To put it better, we are even called to share with God the work of *creating* the truth of our identity. We can evade this responsibility by playing with masks, and this pleases us because it can appear at times to be a free and creative way of living. It is quite easy, and it seems to please everyone. But in the long run the cost and the sorrow come very high. To work out our own identity in God, which the Bible calls "working out our salvation" is a labor that requires sacrifice and anguish, risk and many tears. It demands close attention to reality at every moment, and great fidelity to God as He reveals himself, obscurely, in the mystery of each new situation.[30]

Leach and Paterson believe in the possibility that a supervisee may enter into a personal relationship with God during the

---

30. Merton, *New Seeds of Contemplation*, 32.

supervision process. One of the exercises in which they say this can happen is "Six-minute journaling."[31] This exercise is presented at the end of chapter 4. They recommend, "Treat it as an act of discernment, expecting that God will reveal something to you as you write or reflect afterwards."[32]

Attentive

Within the Christian tradition, the virtue of humility was often praised in the past. Merton is critical of a naive use of this term. He emphasizes that this virtue only becomes relevant after one has had the opportunity to develop one's own mature identity. If representatives of the church do not take this condition into account and, despite this, incite people to humility, this can be regarded as an abuse of power.

At the same time, it remains useful for Merton to think about humility. It is particularly useful if you want to distance yourself from a false self that is one-sidedly aimed at self-affirmation or that wants to conform in a superficial way to ecclesiastical or social standards.

> Humility and consolation go together, for humility is truth experienced in its concrete and existential factuality in our own life. One who simply "runs his own life" by putting into effect ideal projects designed to establish his own ego-image more and more firmly, cannot possibly taste "consolation from God". He is not debarred from other consolations—those which come from the image he has constructed for himself! But these consolations are laborious fabrications, ambivalent and nauseating to anyone with a sense of truth.[33]

Leach and Paterson place pastoral supervision within a church context. They do this from an ecumenical point of view. It is important that supervisees are supported so that they can fulfill their role

---

31. Leach and Paterson, *Pastoral Supervision*, 107–8.
32. Leach and Paterson, *Pastoral Supervision*, 108.
33. Merton, *Contemplation in a World*, 286.

in a mature way within their ecclesiastical and social context. This means, among other things, that they learn to take a critical look at the effect that their professional actions have on others.

PASTORAL SUPERVISION IS NOT

Spiritual Accompaniment

> So, therefore, I would say that it is very important in the contemplative life *not to overemphasize the contemplation*. If we constantly overemphasize these things to which access is inevitably quite rare, we overlook the ordinary authentic real experiences of everyday life as real things to enjoy, things to be happy about, things to praise God for. But the ordinary realities of everyday life, the faith and love with which we live our normal human lives, provide the foundation on which we build those higher things.[34]

Thomas Merton believes in the importance of spiritual direction. At the same time, he points out that this form of accompaniment should not be reduced to a search for special religious experiences. The contemplative experience of unity with God is a gift, and in no way enforceable. Moreover, this kind of experience is not separate from ordinary life. An authentic, contemplative experience reinforces our commitment to other people. Leach and Paterson assume that it is possible to meet God within the normal working environment. Awareness of this can lighten up when, during a supervision session, one considers a specific moment in one's own professional practice. It may be useful to mention the spiritual dimension of that experience, but it is important to leave space for what cannot be easily put into words.

---

34. Merton, *Contemplation in a World*, 352.

Counseling

> The director is not a psychoanalyst. He should stick to his divinely given mission, and avoid two great mistakes. First, he should not become an amateur in psychotherapy. He should not try to concern himself directly with unconscious drives and emotional problems. He should know enough about them to recognize their presence. He should have a deep respect for man's unconscious, instinctual nature. He should not make the mistake of giving a direction that reinforces unconscious and infantile authoritarian trends. At the same time he should not be too easy and too soothing, giving approval to every whim, no matter how unreasonable. Secondly, he should realize that psychological problems are very real and that when they exist they are beyond the range of his competency. He should not be one of those who derides psychiatry on principle and pretends that all emotional problems can be solved by ascetic means. He should know when to refer someone to a psychiatrist for proper treatment. He should not try to "cure" a neurotic by bluffing him, or jollying him along, still less by jumping on him![35]

In this fragment, Merton reflects on the relationship between spiritual direction and psychotherapy. His vision is based on his own experiences with psychoanalysis. As a spiritual director, it is good to have sufficient insight into psychological processes. Merton is aware of the fact that transfer and countertransference can take place during spiritual direction. At the same time, he emphasizes that a spiritual director may not take over the role of a psychotherapist or psychiatrist and must refer people if necessary. After all, it is irresponsible to reduce every problem that is dealt with to a spiritual or religious problem.

With their book, Leach and Paterson want to offer an alternative for people who do not agree with supervision models that are strongly based on therapeutic frameworks. At the same time, they invite the reader to reflect on a number of psychological processes.

---

35. Merton, *Spiritual Direction & Meditation*, 49–50.

In chapter 4 they provide a framework for supervisors to think critically about the interaction between themselves and the supervisees. They are also convinced that pastoral supervision and psychotherapy should not be confused.

Line Management

> The silence of the woods forces you to make a decision which the tensions and artificialities of society may help you to evade forever. Do you want to be yourself or don't you? Do you insist on fighting the images of other people? Must you continue to live as a symbolic appendance to somebody you desire or hate? Are you going to stand on your own feet before God and the world and take full responsibility for your own life?[36]

Merton was convinced that it is difficult for someone in the middle of professional life to look at it from a critical distance. When he lived the last years of his life as a hermit, he remained in contact with the world outside the abbey through correspondence, visits, retreats, and lectures. He invited people not to naively identify with ecclesiastical and social structures. At the same time, he pointed out that it is not easy to criticize these structures because people are situated within them. He was concerned as to know how to relate to these structures in an honest way, and from there how to commit himself as a monk and pastoral practitioner to the changes within the church and society.

For Leach and Paterson, in some circumstances, a line manager may take on the role of supervisor. However, this is not at all self-evident. When a line manager chooses to do so, it is important to think about it with his or her supervisor in order to avoid role confusion and exercise power in an ill-considered manner. By being in supervision, one can take responsibility for one's own actions as a supervisor and manager.

---

36. Merton, *Contemplation in a World*, 245.

Open to the Full Dimension

PASTORAL SUPERVISION AS ATTENTION

Thomas Merton approaches theology from a contemplative and prophetic perspective. Listening to the voice of God is not self-evident. It presupposes that one is prepared to reflect carefully about moments in everyday life. It is important to take ourselves fully serious as relational beings. We are related to nature, to other people, and to our cultural context. It is only by listening attentively to what this multiple context tells us that we can find the voice of God in an authentic way.

> The voice of God is not clearly heard at every moment; and part of the "work of the cell" is attention, so that one may not miss any sound of that voice. What it means, therefore, is not only attention to inner grace but to external reality and to one's self as completely integrated part of that reality. Hence, it implies also a forgetfulness of oneself as totally apart from other objects, standing back from outer objects; it demands an integration of one's own self in the stream of natural and human and cultural life of the moment. When we understand how little we listen, how stubborn and gross our hearts are, we realize how important this inner work is. And we see how badly prepared we are to do it.[37]

In chapter 3, Leach and Paterson show how a praxis situation can be interpreted theologically within pastoral supervision. In her article on theological reflection, Leach describes pastoral theology as attention.[38] She developed her method for theological reflection together with students in the United Kingdom and South Africa.

Merton held extensive correspondence. He saw this as a concretion of his monastic vocation. From 1960 until his death in 1968 he exchanged beautiful letters with the Pakistani Sufi Abdul Aziz. At the request of Aziz, Merton reflects on his personal prayer life in one of his letters. Both in daily life and in prayer it is about

---

37. Merton, *Vow of Conversation*, 189.
38. Leach, "Pastoral Theology as Attention."

attention. Merton testifies how letting go of the false self and discovering the true self ultimately go back to God's liberating action. His reflection shows that Merton has a deep respect for Islam. His familiarity with Sufism helps him to give words to his personal prayer life.

> Strictly speaking I have a very simple way of prayer. It is centered entirely on attention to the presence of God and to His will and His love. That is to say that it is centered on *faith* by which alone we can know the presence of God. One might say this gives my meditation the character described by the Prophet as "being before God as if you saw Him." Yet it does not mean imagining anything or conceiving a precise image of God, for to my mind this would be a kind of idolatry. On the contrary, it is a matter of adoring Him as invisible and infinitely beyond our comprehension, and realizing Him as all. My prayer tends very much toward what you call *fana*. There is in my heart this great thirst to recognize totally the nothingness of all that is not God. My prayer is then a kind of praise rising up out of the center of Nothing and Silence. If I am still present "myself" this I recognize as an obstacle about which I can do nothing unless He Himself removes the obstacle. If He wills He can then make the Nothingness into a total clarity.[39]

During her stay in South Africa, Leach discovered how the students related her methodology for theological reflection to their prayer life.[40] By thinking about the questions in a group, they prayerfully went in search of the will of God in their specific professional situation.

PASTORAL SUPERVISION AS TRANSFORMATION

As a novice master, Thomas Merton thought about how the policy and the liturgy within the abbey could be attuned to the needs of new generations of novices. He realized that a superficial reform

39. Merton, *Hidden Ground of Love*, 63–64.
40. Leach, "Pastoral Theology as Attention."

Open to the Full Dimension

of monastic life would not suffice. In thinking about this, he found it important to go back to the Bible and the patristic tradition. He was interested in looking at this issue interactively and with a broad awareness, from different perspectives. Thinking about the contemplative life for him was not possible without a broadening of consciousness.

> A merely external practice of silence and enclosure will never do anything by itself to guarantee the inner transformation of consciousness which the contemplative life requires. We have to re-examine all our practices with a serious willingness that our present conceptions may simply be inadequate. They need to be made much deeper, and much more alive—and perhaps given an entirely new perspective.[41]

In their Preface and throughout the book, Leach and Paterson focus on the transformative character of pastoral supervision. They refer to Nicki Weld, who challenges supervisees "to reach deeply into themselves and connect with the wider human consciousness that supports them in the work they do."[42]

Thomas Merton situates the concept of transformation within his thinking about the false and the true self. It does not encourage people who are active in pastoral care to give up their social commitment. It is a question of discovering through one's own actions and contemplative reflection on them, who one is meant to be in the deepest sense, and, on this basis, giving a new and deeper interpretation to the roles one takes on in the church and in society.

> The death and crucifixion of the old self, the routine man of self-seeking and conventionally social life, leads to the resurrection in Christ of a totally "new man" who is "one spirit" with Christ. This new man is not just the old man in possession of a legal certificate entitling him to a reward. He is no longer the same, and his reward is precisely this transformation that makes him no longer the isolated subject of a limited award but "one

---

41. Merton, *Contemplation in a World*, 97.
42. Weld, *Practical Guide to Transformative Supervision*, 115.

with Christ" and, in Christ, with all men. The purpose of discipline is then not only to help us "turn on" and understand the inner dimension of existence, but to transform us in Christ in such a way that we completely transcend our routine existence. (Yet in transcending it, we rediscover its existential value and solidity. Transformation is not a repudiation of ordinary life but its definitive recovery in Christ.)[43]

Paterson sees pastoral supervision as an invitation to "vocational regeneration."[44] Leach and Paterson refer in their Preface to Mary Creaner, who describes supervision as "an inside-out rediscovery of what I always knew to be true for myself."[45]

PASTORAL SUPERVISION AS NON-VIOLENT ACTION

Thomas Merton confirms that the concept of incarnation is relevant for theological reflection on pastoral practice. At the same time, he gives a contemporary interpretation to the concept of eschatology. Both concepts must be kept in balance with each other He bases his interpretation of the concept of eschatology on Rudolf Bultmann.[46] He emphasizes the importance of this concept as an existential and pastoral one. It helps Christians to focus on peace building and nonviolent action in their own life.

> The concept of realized eschatology is very important. It means the transformation of life and of human relations by Christ *now* (rather than an eschatology focused on future cosmic and religious events—the Jewish poetic figures which emphasize the transcendence of the Son of Man). Realized eschatology is at the heart of genuine Christian (incarnational) humanism and hence its tremendous importance for the Christian peace effort,

---

43. Merton, *Contemplation in a World*, 99–100.
44. Paterson, "From Therapeutic Leftovers," 16–19.
45. Creaner, "Reflections on Learning," 147.
46. Waldron, *Thomas Merton: Master of Attention*, 52–53.

for example. The presence of the Holy Spirit, the call to repentance, the call to see Christ in man, the presence of the redeeming power of the Cross in the sacraments: these belong to "the last age" in which we now are. But all these do not reveal their significance without a Christian peacemaking mission, without the preaching of the Gospel of unity, non-violence and mercy: the reconciliation of man with man, and therefore with God.[47]

In chapters 6, 7, 8, and 9, Leach and Paterson discuss the concept of incarnation in more detail. This concept can help supervisees to fulfil their assignment in a creative way. Through our physicality we enter into relation with nature, we can express our experiences in symbols and stories and situate ourselves in relation to the social context. In the conclusion of chapter 10, Leach and Paterson summarize their interpretation of the concept of incarnation as follows: "The quality of attentiveness—to the detail of individual situations and contexts; the horizon of God's coming kingdom, to the presence and leading of the Holy Spirit in the here and now—is essential to the authentic incarnation of the body of Christ in our own cultures and time."[48]

Merton thought conscientiously about various forms of social violence that included poverty, war, racism, sexism and colonialism. As a Christian, one cannot pretend that these forms of violence do not exist. In the places where one lives and works, each person is relationally responsible by virtue of one's own vocation. By studying Gandhi's work, the Bible and historical testimonies of peace activists, Merton came to the conclusion that nonviolence unjustly occupies a marginal place in the church and in society. He committed himself to a culture of nonviolence by: engaging in dialogue with nonbelievers, church leaders and peace activists, critically analyzing society, defending the rights of writers and poets in Latin America and by practicing contemplation, fasting, silence, and solitude.

---

47. Merton, *Vow of Conversation*, 31–32.
48. Leach and Paterson, *Pastoral Supervision*, 255–56.

> Nonviolence must be aimed above all at the transformation of the present state of the world, and it must be therefore be free from all occult, unconscious connivance with an unjust use of power. This poses enormous problems—for if nonviolence is too political it becomes drawn into the power struggle and identified with one side or another in that struggle, while if it is totally apolitical it runs the risk of being ineffective or at best merely symbolic.[49]

Based on Thomas Merton, in the context of pastoral supervision but also beyond, the following approaches to non-violence can be fruitful:[50]

- Practicing attention in contact with other people
- To express human experiences and teach others to do the same
- Rejection of excessive activity, of a focus on performance or success
- Practicing contemplation
- Attention to silence that invites conversation
- Resisting consumption
- Learning to lose and let go
- Reading the Holy Scripture
- Maintaining a historical awareness
- Remaining convinced that people are basically good

CONCLUSION

> It's for us to keep our sanity if we possibly can, and to keep a certain amount of lucidity and a genuine fidelity to God's call. Let us keep alive especially the awareness of what is really authentic within our own experience, because we know, we have experienced in moments of

---

49. Merton, *Passion for Peace*, 253.
50. Padovano, *Retreat with Thomas Merton*, 79–82.

Open to the Full Dimension

prayer, in moments of truth and realization, what God really asks of us and what He really wishes to give us. Let us remain faithful to that truth and to that experience.[51]

In our new pastoral supervision course, we make extensive use of the book by Leach and Paterson. In addition, we regularly read excerpts from the work of Thomas Merton with the supervisors in training. Afterwards, we discuss various aspects of pastoral supervision with the group. Based on that experience, I have shown in this chapter how Thomas Merton's work can strengthen, broaden, and deepen the vision of Leach and Paterson. From a contemplative and prophetic perspective, pastoral supervision can be described as attention, transformation, and nonviolent action.

---

51. Merton, *Contemplation in a World*, 355.

4

Thomas Merton, Natural Contemplation and Orthodox Pastoral Theology

IN MY WORK AS a pastoral supervisor and educator, I see it as my task to develop a pastoral theological concept for my professional practice. Because I recently changed my job, I had to develop a new concept that could give a foundation to my work. Since October 2018, I have been working as the head of the Centre for Dialogue at Campus Riedberg (CfD) in Frankfurt am Main, Germany.

In September 2020, together with the Albert Schweitzer Foundation for Our Contemporaries, the CfD organized an interdisciplinary discussion evening on utility animals. The speakers were an animal theologian, Dr. Simone Horstmann, and an agricultural engineer, Dr. Maren Heincke. The conversations we had that night inspired me to reflect more on the value of animal theology for my work.

In this chapter, I want to focus on Thomas Merton as an animal theologian. According to the Merton scholars, Małgorzata Poks and Deborah Kehoe, Merton can be seen as an animal

53

Open to the Full Dimension

theologian, as someone who can contribute to the discussions that are held within this field.[1] I will focus on his reading of the Byzantine monk and theologian, Maximus the Confessor (580–662). Maximus used a threefold schema to describe the development of the spiritual life: praxis (active life), natural contemplation, and theology. Merton refers to this schema to focus on the importance of natural contemplation and to appreciate animals as role models for an active life.

Maximus the Confessor gives a classic description of the spiritual life as three successive stages. This way of describing the spiritual life has been strongly criticized by theologians and spiritual scholars.[2] Neglect of the body and the senses, abuse of the natural world, the subordination of women and the devaluation of lay people have been historical results of the ladder and ascent imagery.[3]

Thomas Merton is aware of the negative historical effects of the metaphor of ascent. His strategy is to focus on the positive elements of this threefold schema and to offer a corrective to the negative effects of it. In that way, he stays true to his philosophy of approaching spiritual literature of the past.

> We have to be careful in studying these things: not because we are likely to be led astray by the errors themselves, but because we are apt to make judgments that are too crude both of the nature of error and of the nature of true Christian spirituality. [There is a] danger of drawing very clear lines of demarcation, with all black on one side and all white on the other, [and so a] need for greater discernment.[4]

Merton is known for his interreligious friendships. In this chapter, I describe how Merton discussed the vision of Maximus the Confessor with his friends, Abdul Aziz and Daisetz T. Suzuki.

The orthodox pastoral theologians, Kyprian Kern and Elisabeth Behr-Sigel, also focus on the positive aspects of the threefold

1. Poks, "Lamb Admits Ties"; Kehoe, "Thomas Merton's Ecopoetry."
2. Sheldrake, *Spirituality and History*, 188–89.
3. Miles, *Practicing Christianity*, 78–79.
4. Merton, *Cassian and the Fathers*, 16.

schema of Maximus the Confessor. At the same time, they offer a corrective to the negative effects of the metaphor of ascent. In this chapter, I bring them into dialogue with Thomas Merton. I want to discover what I can learn from their reading of Maximus for my work as pastoral supervisor and educator.

THOMAS MERTON AND ANIMAL THEOLOGY

Regarding manuals on animal theology, one can basically distinguish between two kinds of approaches, namely "seeking a better understanding of either the nonhuman creature, or the human relation to the nonhuman."[5] Within the first approach, Christian animal theologians focus on the Bible, tradition, or on modern scientific understandings of nonhuman animals. Animal theologians who choose the second approach have developed different models of relationship, "including rights based language as well as examinations into particular ethical issues that arise in common human-nonhuman interactions (e.g., the nonhuman as source of food or clothing for humans)."[6]

In this chapter, I want to reflect on Thomas Merton as an animal theologian. I will focus on the first approach within animal theology, specifically on the way Merton looks at how nonhuman animals are presented in the Bible and in tradition. For Merton, this approach is connected to the second one. It helps us to discover how to relate to them in a responsible way.

During the last decade of his life, Thomas Merton was strongly interested in ethical questions regarding nonhuman animals. To illustrate this I refer to his statement on factory farming, which was published in 1965.

> A STATEMENT ON FACTORY FARMING
> Since factory farming exerts a violent and unnatural force upon the living organisms of animals and birds, in order to increase production and profits, and since it

---

5. Hiuser, *Animals, Theology and the Incarnation*, 4.
6. Hiuser, *Animals, Theology and the Incarnation*, 4.

involves callous and cruel exploitation of life, with implicit contempt for nature and for life, I must join the protest which is being uttered against it. It does not seem that these methods have any really justifiable purpose except to increase the quantity of production at the expense of quality: if that can be called a justifiable purpose. However, this is only one aspect of a more general phenomenon: the increasingly destructive and irrational behavior of technological man. Our society seems to be more and more oriented to overproduction, to waste, and finally to production for destruction. Its orientation to global war is the culminating absurdity of its inner logic, or lack of logic. The mistreatment of animals in "intensive husbandry" is then part of this larger picture of insensitivity to genuine values and indeed to humanity and to life itself—a picture which more and more seems to display the ugly lineaments of what can only be called by its right name: barbarism.[7]

THOMAS MERTON AND MAXIMUS THE CONFESSOR

Through the last two decades of his life, Merton developed a keen interest in the writings of the Byzantine monk and theologian, Maximus the Confessor (580–662). Maximus's work can be classified in three genres: gnostic centuries, question and answer, and commentary.[8] Merton was reading Maximus's work in *The Philokalia* and studied two of his spiritual works intensively: *Ascetic Live* and *Four Centuries on Love*.[9]

Merton was familiar with the scholarly literature on Maximus the Confessor. He was very excited about the work of the Orthodox theologian, Vladimir Lossky, a professor at Saint-Denys Institute

---

7. Quoted in Weis, "Prophetic Merton," 12.
8. Louth, *Maximus the Confessor*, 20–21; Tollefsen, *Christocentric Cosmology*, 4–6.
9. See Palmer, *Philokalia*; Merton, *St. Maximus the Confessor*; Maxime Le Confesseur, *Centuries sur la Charité*; Maximus the Confessor, *Ascetic Life*.

in Paris. In his classic book, *The Mystical Theology of the Eastern Church*, Lossky referred extensively to Maximus the Confessor.[10] Through his friend Donald Allchin, an Anglican priest with a keen interest in Orthodox theology, Merton received the first edition of a book written by the Scandinavian Maximus scholar Lars Thunberg.[11] The second edition of Thunberg's book, *Microcosm and Mediator*,[12] is considered to be one of the best books ever written on Maximus in the English language.[13] Merton was familiar with other Maximus scholars, Hans Urs von Balthasar and Irénée Hausherr (pseudonym: J. Lemaitre).

From 1951 till 1955, Thomas Merton was Master of Scholastics at the Abbey of Gethsemani. In 1954, Merton presented a course to his students for priesthood, "Sanctity in the Epistles of Saint Paul."[14] In his lecture notes, one can find four pages on Saint Maximus.[15] From 1955 till 1965, Thomas Merton was Master of Novices. In 1961, Merton was asked to teach a pastoral course for newly ordained priests, *An Introduction to Christian Mysticism*. In this course, one can find a fifteen-page chapter on Maximus the Confessor, "Contemplation and the Cosmos."[16] In these two courses, one can see how Merton gradually developed his approach to animal theology based on his reading of the Bible and tradition.

MAXIMUS THE CONFESSOR AND "SANCTITY IN THE EPISTLES OF SAINT PAUL"

In the 1954 notes, Merton translated and summarized the last chapter of the French version of the first edition of Balthasar's

---

10. Lossky, *Mystical Theology*.
11. Thunberg, *Microcosm and Mediator*.
12. Thunberg, *Microcosm and Mediator* (2nd ed.).
13. Louth, *Wisdom of Byzantine Church*, 19.
14. Kilcourse, *Ace of Freedoms*, 244–45.
15. Merton, "Sanctity in the Epistles," 21–25.
16. Merton, *Introduction to Mysticism*, 121–36.

Open to the Full Dimension

book: *Liturgie Cosmique*.[17] To present the basic ideas of Maximus, Merton quoted *Chapters on Knowledge* (1.66).[18]

> The mystery of the Incarnation of the Word contains in itself the force and meaning of all the challenging puzzles and symbols of Scripture, as well as the significant content of all visible and intelligible creatures. Whoever understands the mystery of the Cross and the grave has grasped the essential content (*logos*) of all the things that we have mentioned; and whoever, in addition, has been initiated into the mysterious meaning and power of the Resurrection knows the primordial (*prongoumenos*) purpose for which God created the universe.[19]

According to Maximus, the Word (*Logos*), the second person of the Trinity, is incarnated in three ways: in the creation, in Scripture and in Jesus Christ.[20] To understand the meaning of these incarnations, human beings must look at them with contemplative eyes. Maximus uses a threefold schema developed by Evagrius Ponticus (345–399), to help us understand how we can relate to these incarnations in a contemplative way: praxis (active life), natural contemplation, and theology.

Merton refers to this threefold schema in his notes without mentioning Evagrius. In it, he summarizes a fragment in which Balthasar makes an analysis of *Difficulties in Sacred Scripture* 27. In this chapter, Maximus gives an interpretation of Acts 10:9–16.

> The sheet signifies the sensible world, composed of four principles, as if from four elements, by which it is also governed. The reptiles, wild animals, and birds of the air represent the different inner principles of the things that have been brought into being, principles that are unclean as regards sense perception, but in themselves are clean and nutritious and sustain intelligible life. The voice

---

17. Balthasar, *Liturgie Cosmique*.
18. See Maximus Confessor, *Selected Writings*, 139–40.
19. Quoted in Balthasar, *Liturgie Cosmique*, 210. Also in Balthasar, *Cosmic Liturgy*, 278.
20. Thunberg, *Microcosm and Mediator* (2nd ed.), 77.

heard three times respectively teaches practical, natural, and theological philosophy.[21]

It is interesting to note that Maximus describes creatures as clean and nutritious in themselves. Merton sees it as typical for the Bible and the patristic tradition to consider creation as something good.

> When the New Testament speaks of the "World", it speaks not of God's creation (which God saw from the very beginning to be "very good") but of the division in God's creation brought about by man's spirit of selfishness and dissension.[22]

In his book, *The New Man*, which was based on his reading in the early fifties of Balthasar and other patristic scholars, Merton shows how the active life, natural contemplation, and theology relate to each other reciprocally.

> Although Adam was first of all a contemplative, Genesis seems to place all the stress on his *active life* in Paradise. In Paradise there was no opposition between action and contemplation. We too, if we recover, in Christ, the paradisiacal life of Adam which He has restored to us, are supposed to discover that the opposition between them vanishes at last. Therefore it is interesting to consider Adam at work in the Garden of Eden, and find out that even his activity had an essentially contemplative character, since it was entirely impregnated with light and significance by his union with God. "The Lord God," says Genesis (2:15), "took the man and placed him in the Garden of Eden to till it and keep it." The sentence is as deeply mysterious as any other in this wonderful text. In the first place we might expect it to have a spiritual sense, in which the meaning would be that Adam's main task would be to preserve his own union with God, his own perfect and original contact with reality as its source. However, the Fathers interpreted it literally, since from

---

21. Maximos the Confessor, *Difficulties in Sacred Scripture*, 184–85.
22. Merton, *Monastic Peace*, 4.

Open to the Full Dimension

the start man was to act as God's instrument in cultivating and developing the natural creation.[23]

In his notes on Maximus, Merton stressed that "the perfect Christian" fulfills a liturgical role while gathering creation before God through active life, natural contemplation and theology. In *Bread in the Wilderness*, Merton describes the way that King David took up this role.

> David is drunk with the love of God and filled with the primitive sense that man is the *Leitourgos* or the high priest of all creation, born with the function of uttering in "liturgy" the whole testimony of praise which mute creation cannot of itself offer to its God.[24]

The patristic scholar Andrew Louth describes how, according to Maximus, human beings can take up their role as priests of creation through a praxis of virtue (active life) and natural contemplation.

> This entails that the personal life of struggle against temptation, and growing in virtue, is not simply a personal matter, what Michel Foucault called *"souci de soi"*, care for the self, it is a matter of cosmic significance, for such ascetic struggle restores the human capacity for being priest of nature, interpreter of the cosmos. This is true for Maximos in various ways, but one that is immediately relevant here is that through ascetic struggle the Christian attains a state of serenity, and one of the fruits of that serenity is to be able to see the *logoi* of creation: to see the cosmos as God intended it, to have our capacity for spiritual sight restored.[25]

In a similar fashion, Merton stressed in his notes of 1954, the ascetic struggle of the "perfect Christian." As priests of creation, human beings are able to see the *logoi* of creation. In that way, they are different from nonhuman animals. At the same time, Merton stressed that the whole creation will be saved in the end.

---

23. Merton, *New Man*, 77–78.
24. Merton, *Bread in Wilderness*, 57.
25. Louth, "Between Creation and Transfiguration," 219.

Thomas Merton, Natural Contemplation and Orthodox Pastoral Theology

MAXIMUS THE CONFESSOR AND *AN INTRODUCTION TO CHRISTIAN MYSTICISM*

In 1961, Merton did teach a pastoral course for newly ordained priests, *An Introduction to Christian Mysticism*. In this course, he exhaustively spoke about Maximus the Confessor and the importance of natural contemplation (*theoria physike*). Merton shows how Maximus makes use of the threefold schema of Evagrius. At the same time, he stresses that Maximus's take on this schema is very original.

> We can in fact say that the lack of *theoria physike* is one of the things that accounts for the stunting of spiritual growth among our monks today. On the contrary, where there is a genuine growth from the serenity of at least a relative *apatheia* to the enriched state of *gnosis* by "natural contemplation," then we are fully and integrally prepared for *theologia* without forms, beyond all ideas and symbols.[26]

Different from the course Merton gave in 1954, the focus here is not so much on the "perfect Christian," but on pastoral praxis and the relation to society. To show the relevance of natural contemplation for pastoral practitioners, Merton brings this topic in dialogue with different aspects of our society: natural sciences, technology, arts and work.

In *The Inner Experience*, a book that is closely related to the pastoral course, Merton gives a remarkable description of natural contemplation.[27]

> *Theoria physike* is contemplation of the divine *in nature*, not contemplation of the divine *by our natural powers*. And in fact, "natural contemplation" in this sense is mystical: that is to say, it is a gift from God, a divine enlightenment. But it still involves labor and preparation on the part of the contemplative. He has to look about him, see the created world and the symbols with which it is filled.

26. Merton, *Introduction to Mysticism*, 121.
27. See Foltz, *Noetics of Nature*, 174.

He *has to* receive, in the sign language of Scripture and Liturgy, words of God which transform his inner life. Natural contemplation, according to the Greek Fathers, also "sees" and communes with the angelic beings who form a part of created nature. This natural contemplation, which beholds the divine in and through nature, has served me as a prototype for what I have chosen to call "active contemplation"—a contemplation which man seeks and prepares by his own initiative but which, by a gift from God, is completed in *mystical intuition*.[28]

Reflecting on natural contemplation in relation to nonhuman animals, Merton refers to *Difficulties in Sacred Scripture 27*, and stresses their goodness.[29] In *Difficulties in Sacred Scripture 51*, Maximus argues that nonhuman animals can be an inspiration for humans to act in a responsible way towards other humans and towards the creation.[30]

> St. Maximus says we must be attuned not only to the *logoi* of creatures but also to *tropoi* or models of action: we get the light from the *logoi*, we get order and love from the *tropoi*. They not only move us to praise but they guide us in action. It is very important to realize that *theoria physike* is actually a dynamic unity of contemplation and action.[31]

According to Maximus, nonhuman animals can be an inspiration for human action. The precondition is that humans look at them from a contemplative perspective. Maximus illustrates this in *Difficulties in Sacred Scripture 51*, in which he makes an exegesis of 2 Chr 32:23. He uses his take on the threefold schema of Evagrius to make his interpretation of the text.

> In this way, then, the supremely philosophical mind comes with knowledge to the sources of created beings by the natural principle (*logos*) and mode (*tropos*) of each

---

28. Merton, *Inner Experience*, 68.
29. Merton, *Introduction to Mysticism*, 128.
30. Lemaitre, "Contemplation," 1817.
31. Merton, *Introduction to Mysticism*, 129.

thing. Insofar as it is gnostic (*gnostikos*), it receives, like "gifts," the spiritual principles of created beings, offered by the creation. Insofar as it is practical (*praktikos*), it receives "donations" when it imitates the natural laws of created beings in its own conduct. It reveals in itself, by its way of life, all the magnificence of the divine wisdom contained invisibly in created things.[32]

THOMAS MERTON, MAXIMUS THE CONFESSOR AND INTERRELIGIOUS DIALOGUE

Thomas Merton is known for his ministry of friendship.[33] One way for him to realize this ministry was to exchange letters with people from different religious traditions. In a letter to Abdul Aziz, a Muslim friend from Pakistan, on September 24, 1961, he writes about natural contemplation.

> This is an aspect of mysticism that I have not studied so much: that of the intermediate realm of what the Greek Fathers called *Theoria Physike* (natural contemplation) which deals with the symbols and images of things and their character as words or manifestations of God the Creator, whose Wisdom is in them.[34]

On March 12, 1959, Merton started a correspondence with the famous Zen scholar, Daisetz T. Suzuki. In that same year, they collaborated in a dialogue which was later published in *Zen and the Birds of Appetite*.[35] In their correspondence, Merton discussed the Christian meaning of paradise.

> Your intuition about paradise is profoundly correct and patristic. In Christ the world and the whole cosmos has been created anew (which means to say restored to its original perfection and beyond that made divine, totally

---

32. Quoted in Blowers, *Exegesis and Spiritual Pedagogy*, 145.
33. Merton, *Life in Letters*, xi–xii.
34. Merton, *Hidden Ground of Love*, 50.
35. Merton, *Zen and the Birds*.

Open to the Full Dimension

transfigured). The whole world has risen in Christ, say the Fathers. If God is "all in all," then everything is in fact paradise, because it is filled with the glory and presence of God, and nothing is any more separated from God.[36]

In their dialogue, Merton discussed Evagrius and Maximus and their different approach to the threefold schema of praxis, natural contemplation and theology.

> It is the *quies*, or rest, of contemplation—the state of being free from all images and concepts which disturb and occupy the soul. It is the favorable climate for *theologia*, the highest contemplation, which excludes even the purest and most spiritual of ideas and admits no concepts whatever. It knows God not by concepts and visions, but only by "unknowing". This is the language of Evagrius Ponticus, severely intellectual, a fact which brings him closer to Zen than the more affective theologians of prayer like St. Maximus and St. Gregory of Nyssa.[37]

MERTON'S CRITIQUE OF MAXIMUS THE CONFESSOR

It is important for Merton to look at nonhuman animals from a contemplative perspective. He considers the threefold schema from Evagrius and the way it was developed by Maximus as very helpful. It helps him focus on the importance of the active life and natural contemplation for a mature spirituality.

At the same time, he agrees that in today's context the metaphor of ascent cannot be used in a naïve way. One cannot ignore the historical result of this threefold schema: a suspicion of the body and the senses, the destruction and neglect of the natural world, the subordination of women, and a devaluation of lay people in the church.[38]

36. Merton, *Hidden Ground of Love*, 563–64.
37. Merton, *Zen and the Birds*, 131.
38. Miles, *Practicing Christianity*, 78–79.

Merton questions the way Maximus uses his threefold schema to analyze the presentation of nonhuman animals in the Bible. Merton stresses the metaphorical quality of these representations. Maximus reduces the richness of these metaphors because he only looks at them in a schematic way.

> The mind imitates the deer when, for example, it pursues the highest mountains of divine speculations; and destroys, by the principle of discretion, the passions which lurk like poisonous animals in the nature of created beings; and dispels, through numerous and diverse sources of knowledge, the poison of evil that is confined in its memory through adversity.[39]

In the last decade of Merton's life, his environmental consciousness expanded.[40] Reading his journals in the period when he moved to the hermitage, one can discover how important it was for him to experience the beauty of nonhuman animals through his body and senses. For Merton, natural contemplation was a way of everyday seeing.

> Last evening when the moon was rising saw the warm burning soft red of a doe in the field. It was still light enough so I got the field glasses and watched her. Presently a stag came out, and then I saw a second doe and, briefly, another stag. They were not afraid. Looked at me from time to time. I watched their beautiful running, grazing. Everything, every movement was completely lovely, but there is a kind of gaucheness about them sometimes that makes them even lovelier. The thing that struck me most: one sees, looking at them directly in movement, just what the cave painters saw—something that I have never seen in a photograph. It is an awe-inspiring thing—the *Mantu* or "spirit" shown in the running of the deer, the "deerness" that sums up everything and is saved and marvelous. A contemplative intuition! Yet perfectly, ordinary, everyday seeing. The deer reveals something essential in myself! Something beyond the

---

39. Quoted in Blowers, *Exegesis and Spiritual Pedagogy*, 144.
40. Weis, *Environmental Vision*; Weis, "Merton's Fascination."

trivialities of my everyday being, and my individuality. The stags much darker, mouse-grey, or rather a warm grey brown like a flying squirrel. I could sense the softness of their coat and longed to touch them.[41]

THOMAS MERTON, MAXIMUS THE CONFESSOR AND KYPRIAN KERN

Merton was interested in the theological work that was done by the Orthodox theologians at St. Sergius Institute in Paris. He studied the work of Sergius Bulgakov, Paul Evdokimov, Alexander Schmemann, John Meyendorff, and others.[42] As far as I can see, he was not familiar with the work of the pastor and theologian Kyprian Kern (1900–1960). The explanation for this seems to be rather obvious. Kern wrote in Russian and Merton had only a basic knowledge of that language. During his lifetime, only a fraction of the work of Kern was published in French or English.

Kyprian Kern joined the St. Sergius Institute in 1937, first as professor of liturgy and then, since 1940, as professor of patristics. He was also a pastoral theologian. He did teach a course in Orthodox pastoral ministry. His major works are: *Flowers of Prayer (Essays in Liturgical Theology*; 1928), *Archmandrite Antonine Kapoustine, Head of the Russian Mission in Jerusalem* (1936), *The Eucharist* (1947), *Anthropology of St. Gregory Palamas* (1950), *Orthodox Pastoral Ministry* (1957). Through his research on Gregory Palamas, he had a major influence on John Meyendorff.[43] The sacramental and pastoral theology of Alexander Schmemann was also strongly influenced by the work and teaching of Kyprian Kern.[44] In the last years of his life, Kern was the organizer and mentor of

---

41. Merton, *Learning to Love*, 291.

42. Merton, "Orthodoxy and the World." For an excellent analysis of Thomas Merton and Orthodox theology, see Pramuk, *Sophia*.

43. Russell, *Gregory Palamas*, 77.

44. Mills, *Church, World, and Kingdom*, 18.

the "St. Sergius Liturgical Conferences." These conferences were strongly ecumenical in character. In an article on the theology of Gregory Palamas, published in French by the Belgian ecumenical monastery of Chevetogne, Kern referred to the threefold schema of praxis, natural contemplation and theology in the way it was developed by Pseudo-Dionysius the Areopagite and Maximus. He stressed that every Christian can go up the path of ascent.

> The knowledge of God is by no means clear, and it is through mystical intuition and, as with the author of the *Celestial Hierarchy*, corresponds to an inner maturation and degrees of spiritual growth. "For this, purification of the heart and pious boldness are necessary above all." The Christian can then rise from the first degree of a simple believer to that of the disciple and up to that of the apostle. It is the way of active victory over the passions, the way of a gradual ascent, then of entry into darkness, "into one of enlightenment, deprived of all forms and things like Moses." In the face of such an approach to the source of light, God reveals Himself as He really is, supra-substantial and incomprehensible Spirit. This is why for Maximus, "God makes himself known not according to His essence but according to the magnificence of His creatures, and His providence towards them. We see His grace, His wisdom, His strength, reflected in them like a mirror."[45]

In a similar fashion as Merton, Kern argues in his course on Orthodox pastoral ministry that Maximus and the patristic tradition see the creation as good.

> For all its richness and glory, there is only one word in the Greek language—cosmos—to describe "world" and "beauty." Creation, even if fallen, is of divine origin. It was already in existence in God's divine plan for the world. This event, this Godly structure of the world is the reflection of a different reality, not empirical, which gives rich material for the "symbolic realism" of the Holy Fathers and abundant means for deeper contemplation

45. Kern, "Les Eléments de la Théologie," 12–13.

Open to the Full Dimension

of the world as well as our selves. Only through divine origin can creation be blessed and undergo transfiguration. If the world itself is evil, this would mean that it was created evil. But evil, as thought by Maximus the Confessor, is not the natural essence characteristic of creation, but its foolish and sinful usage.[46]

According to Kern, such a contemplative creation theology has immediate consequences for pastoral practice. He refers to an old patristic debate regarding the true nature of Jesus Christ. This debate seems to live on today because of the aversion of human beings towards the rest of creation.

> Christianity defeated Monophysitism, but as a Western historian correctly pointed out, it did not overcome the famous "psychological monophysitism." This "psychological monophysitism," this human and worldly aversion to acknowledge God's creation, throws a thin, yet strong cloud over asceticism, literature, liturgy, and ethics of Christianity. The pastor must understand this and firmly oppose it. One must always bear in mind the resolution of the Gangra Council, condemning excessive asceticism and pseudo-pious Puritanism which have no place in the strict Orthodox world-view; this, then, must be the cosmological basis for pastorship.[47]

Based on the Bible and his interpretation of the patristic tradition, Merton uses a similar tone. The destruction and dominion of creation is related to a hard and rigid faith, which is the product of conventionalism and systematic prejudice.

> The man of faith is ideally free from prejudice and plastic in his uninhibited response to each new movement of the stream of life. I say "ideally" in order to exclude those whose faith is not pure but is also another form of prejudice enthroned in the exterior man—a preconceived opinion rather than a living responsiveness to the *logos* of each new situation. For there exists a kind of "hard" and rigid religious faith that is not really alive or

46. Kern, *Orthodox Pastoral Service*, 16.
47. Kern, *Orthodox Pastoral Service*, 17.

spiritual, but resides entirely in the exterior self and is a product of conventionalism and systematic prejudice.[48]

In a classic article published in 1937, Kern presented two models of ministry: "levitical" and "prophetic."[49] This article was written in a period when Fascism and nationalism were on the rise in Europe. Kern was reflecting on the social responsibility of pastors in such a context.

> In saying "levite" or "prophet" I thus presume, so to say, to describe a pastoral style. A levitical and a pastoral designation in this case is used to define specific categories of spirituality. These are not institutions of religious practice but are religious and psychological types.[50]

A levitical style of ministry is ritualistic, nationalistic, and conventional. A prophetic style of ministry is creative, transnational, and has a compassionate openness to God's creation.

> The priesthood of the levitical tradition, in other words, has fallen into a deep slumber. It fell asleep even before the Divine *Logos* ascended upon the earth and it has neither awakened nor was it capable of hearing how that *Logos*, having become incarnate, proclaimed a new Truth and a new commandment for all people—and most certainly and primarily for the pastors, who are called to carry out that commandment.[51]

Many years later, based on his reading of the prophets, the New Testament, and the signs of the times, Merton criticizes in a similar way, a nationalistic and collectivistic kind of religion.

> In other words, Jesus foresees the end of a world that is fragmented and divided, and in which each division or fragment asserts its identity by special rites in honor of a special god. The God to whom the "religious" man cries as "my God" has hitherto been the God of his tribe,

48. Merton, *Inner Experience*, 56.
49. Valliere, *Modern Russian Theology*, 391–92.
50. Kern, "Two Models," 110.
51. Kern, "Two Models," 116.

69

his nation, his king. Hence the "my God" of tribal or national religion is by definition not "their God"—he is *for* us and *against* everyone else. If "religion" only exists in order to establish this peculiar emphasis on one's collective identity, than it is indeed rendered obsolete by the universalism of the prophets and of the apostles.[52]

Human beings can only be priests of creation when they, through active life and contemplation, give up their tribal claims and rituals and discover Gods intention within human history and the responsibility they have towards creation.

THOMAS MERTON, MAXIMUS THE CONFESSOR, AND ELIZABETH BEHR-SIGEL

Merton was concerned about the subordination of women and the devaluation of lay people in the church. Traditionally, the priest and the monk were seen as a higher class, based on the metaphors of the ladder and the ascent. Merton has an objection towards a church with two classes in common with the orthodox pastoral theologian, Elisabeth Behr-Sigel.

Thomas Merton had a keen interest in the theology prevalent at St. Sergius Institute. As far as I can see, he did not know Elisabeth Behr-Sigel (1907–2005). She was a French pastor, peace activist, and theologian who was very well-known in ecumenical circles in Europe and beyond. She did teach a correspondence course in ascetic theology at Saint-Sergius in 1981. Behr-Sigel regretted that as a woman, she did not have the chance to become a professor at this Institute.[53] This did not prevent her being in a constructive and critical dialogue with the scholars at St. Sergius, especially Sergius Bulgakov, and Paul Evdokimov.[54] In the second half of her professional career, she focused on the ordination of women in the Orthodox Church.

---

52. Merton, *Opening the Bible*, 87–88.
53. Lossky, *Toward the Endless Day*, 201.
54. Wilson, *Woman, Women, and Priesthood*.

Thomas Merton, Natural Contemplation and Orthodox Pastoral Theology

In her course on ascetical theology, she gave a description of the threefold schema of Evagrius: praxis, natural contemplation, and theology. She was critical regarding Catholic patristic scholars such as Hans Urs von Balthasar and Irénée Hausherr who saw Evagrius as the father of Hesychasm. They questioned the Christian character of his mysticism and reduced it to the level of pure abstraction.

> *Theôria physikè* is a logical knowledge of beings according to their "reasons," that is their *logoï*, that have their source in the *Logos*; . . . the words "logical," "reasons," that is *logoï*, must be properly understood so as not to lead to any misunderstanding. They do not refer to a rational, intellectual knowledge in the sense of modern science. Knowledge in the *Logos* is a decoding, an unfolding, a displaying of the whole of creation, cosmic, angelic, and human, as well as of creation history, in light of the mystery of Christ.[55]

According to Maximus, the *Logos*, second person of the Trinity, incarnated in a threefold way: in creation, in Scripture, and in Jesus Christ. Through the incarnation of the *Logos* as a concrete human being, all human beings are able to fulfill their priestly role towards creation. Within the field of feminist theology, the particularity of God's incarnation as not merely a human, but as a male human, has been a topic of discussion. It has been described as the "scandal of particularity."[56] If a male human being is normative for finding out what it means to be a priest of creation, one could argue that men are more able than women to take up this role.

Behr-Sigel discussed the topic of Christ being incarnated as a male human in her reflections on the ordination of women within the Orthodox Church. In classic Orthodox theology, the ordained priest is seen as an icon of Christ.[57] Because of that, women cannot become an ordained priest. To criticize this argument against the

---

55. Behr-Sigel, *Place of the Heart*, 68.
56. Rigby, "Scandalous Presence," 58–60.
57. Ladouceur, *Modern Orthodox Theology*, 384–88.

Open to the Full Dimension

ordination of women, Behr-Sigel referred to Maximus and his interpretation of Gal 3:28.[58]

> He drove out from nature the difference and division into male and female, a difference, as I have said, which He in no way needed in order to become man, and without which existence would perhaps have been possible. There is no need for this division to last *perpetually, for in Christ Jesus*, says the divine apostle, *there is neither male or female*.[59]

During a retreat that Merton held for contemplative prioresses at the Abbey of Gethsemani, Merton spoke about the differences between men and women.

> Men stand to gain by the rehabilitation of women; men will be more whole when women are. What everybody has to be is a *person*. Wholeness is in the reciprocity between men and women as persons who have the same nature. Differences are there and these need to be taken into account, but differences are not decisive.[60]

Merton had a conversation with these Catholic prioresses about the ordination of women. He pointed out that he did not want to be seen as an expert on this matter.

> Whether a solution to the problem is for women to be priests, I don't know. I leave that to you to figure out. Mary Daly seems to think it is very important.
> *She thinks it is essential.*
> Right now, I don't see it. In her argument, Marie Daly is considering a masculine form of hierarchical setup and saying that women have to get into this place that men have made for themselves in the hierarchy. I don't think that at all. I think the whole thing needs to be changed, the whole idea of the priesthood has to be changed.[61]

---

58. Karras, "Patristic Gender Anthropology," 76–85.
59. Maximos the Confessor, *Difficulties in Church Fathers*, 41.
60. Merton, *Springs of Contemplation*, 170.
61. Merton, *Springs of Contemplation*, 175.

In the second half of her career, Behr-Sigel developed an inclusive approach to ordained priesthood in which the role of the priest is not reduced to liturgy.[62] For her, there is no ontological difference between the ordained minister and the members of the community.

> Their priesthood, according to Orthodox teaching, is not ontologically different of the priesthood of all the faithful. It is not another essence than theirs. . . . Ordination does not mean promotion to a higher grade in a hierarchy of which the royal priesthood or the so-called "minor" orders are the lower degrees.[63]

In 1967, Thomas Merton wrote a strong statement on clerical celibacy. Like Behr-Sigel, he is also convinced that there cannot be two classes of Christians.

> The notion that priests must be celibate forms part and parcel of a general attitude toward man, the flesh and the world. It implies a down-grading of worldly life, a suspicion of marriage and the flesh, and suggests that the perfect Christian life is that of virgins. This leads to the division of Christians into two classes: those who take their faith most seriously and are consequently celibate, and "second class Christians" who have to marry but who make up for it by trying to maintain some vestiges of a monastic spirituality even in lay life, and bringing up one or two children for the priesthood or the cloister. This idea of Christianity prevailed for centuries and doubtless worked well within the framework of a hierarchical society which has, however, ceased to exist. It is now seriously called into question by theologians who cannot be ignored.[64]

Behr-Sigel stressed in her work the importance of the royal priesthood (1 Pet 2:9). According to Maximus the Confessor, who Behr-Sigel considered as an important resource, the royal

---

62. Wilson, *Woman, Women, and Priesthood*, 92.
63. Behr-Sigel, *Meaning of Ministry*, 96–97.
64. Merton, "Statement on Clerical Celibacy."

Open to the Full Dimension

priesthood can be realized by taking up our role as priests of creation.[65] The ordained priest, man or women, has a pastoral responsibility to nourish and strengthen fellow human beings to take up that role.

> The "fear" and "trembling" are always surmounted by a confident hope and desire for the ultimate transfiguration of humanity and the entire cosmos, characteristic of Eastern spirituality.[66]

CONCLUSION

In this chapter, I have presented Thomas Merton as an animal theologian. Merton developed his approach to animal theology through his reading of the Bible and the patristic tradition. I focused specifically on his reading of Maximus the Confessor. The threefold schema of praxis, natural contemplation, and theology can help animal theologians and practitioners look at their work from a contemplative perspective.

Merton criticizes Maximus, because he was not able to see the metaphorical richness of representations of nonhuman animals in the Bible. Based on his own experiences, Merton invites us to look at them with a contemplative eye and to commit ourselves to the protection of the environment.

Deeply rooted in his own tradition, Merton engaged himself in a ministry of friendship. His aim was to step into a mutual learning process. The correspondence with his Muslim friend, Abdul Aziz, and the Zen scholar, Daisetz T. Suzuki, shows how Merton deepened his reflections on the relationship between active life and natural contemplation and placed them within an interreligious context.

Neglect of the body and the senses, abuse of the natural world, subordination of women and the devaluation of lay people have been historical results of the ladder and ascent imagery.

---

65. Louth, "Between Creation and Transfiguration," 214–20.
66. Behr-Sigel, "Hesychasm and Western Impact," 442.

Thomas Merton, Natural Contemplation and Orthodox Pastoral Theology

Thomas Merton is aware of the negative historical effects of the metaphor of ascent. His strategy is to focus on the positive elements of this threefold schema and to offer a corrective to the negative effects of it.

In this chapter, I brought two Orthodox pastoral theologians, who worked at the St. Sergius Institute in Paris, into conversation with Thomas Merton. Kyprian Kern and Elisabeth Behr-Sigel developed their approach to pastoral theology from the Bible and the patristic tradition.

Kyprian Kern and Thomas Merton invite animal theologians and pastoral practitioners to develop their work from a mystical-prophetic perspective.

Based on Maximus's reading of Gal 3:28, and a broader view on ordained priesthood, Behr-Sigel argued that both men and women can be ordained as priests. Together with Maximus the Confessor and Thomas Merton, Elisabeth Behr-Sigel invites pastoral practitioners to strengthen and nourish fellow human beings to become priests of creation.

5

Thomas Merton and Septima Clark on the Civil Rights Movement and Adult Education

TILL TODAY, THOMAS MERTON is especially known as a spiritual author. People who are more familiar with his work know that he devoted himself considerably to social themes in his later writings: interreligious and intrareligious dialogue, poverty and social exclusion, peace and nonviolence, literature and art, ecology and technology. The combination of non-conformism, attention to spirituality and a strong social commitment in his thinking characterise the person of Thomas Merton and turn him into a figure who can still inspire us today.

In collaboration with the Sisters of Loretto, Merton organized in December 1967 and in May 1968, a retreat for prioresses of contemplative congregations. With this group of women, he talked about their religious and prophetic vocation. During an interview, Mary Luke Tobin, SL said the following about this retreat:

> I think he was like everybody else. It was beginning to dawn on him. The *whole* feminist thing was beginning to

dawn on him. You know one of the books he encouraged to read was a book by Karl Stern wich is called *Flight from Woman*. He read that and said to me, "Oh, you *must* read that book." He read Mary Daly too. Imagine! He was recommending these writers to those nuns. He said, "Now you have to get on to these women." He talked about "feminine mystique." He gave them a whole talk on the "feminine mystique." So I think he was in step with the emerging feminist movement. Nobody knows that about him. But it's true. I experienced it.[1]

In the final decade of his life, Merton was also involved strongly with the African American civil rights movement. Together with June Yungblut, he prepared an encounter with Martin Luther King Jr., Vincent Harding, and Thích Nhất Hạnh in the Abbey of Gethsemani. The assassination of Dr. King, however, saw to it that this retreat could not take place. While the African American civil rights movement engaged itself politically in nonviolence, Merton focused his work on inspirational historical examples like: Mahatma Gandhi, Simone Weil, Alfred Delp, Franz Jägerstätter, and Maximus the Confessor.[2]

Merton linked the struggle of African American citizens with the worldwide emancipation of numerous population groups after colonisation. This broad perspective was also found in well-known and lesser known leaders within the African American civil rights movement. In her book, *Outlaw Culture*, bell hooks says the following:

> The civil rights movement had the power to transform society because the individuals who struggle alone and in community for freedom and justice wanted these gifts to be for all, not just the suffering and the oppressed. Visionary black leaders such as Septima Clark, Fannie Lou Hammer, Martin Luther King Jr., and Howard Thurman warned against isolationism. They encouraged black people to look beyond our own circumstances and assume responsibility for the planet. This call for

---

1. Kramer and Kramer, "Growing in Responsibility," 48.
2. Merton, *Passion for Peace*.

Open to the Full Dimension

communion with a world beyond the self, the tribe, the race, the nation, was a constant invitation for personal expansion and growth.[3]

In this chapter, I reflect on three of Merton's texts. I will search for the contemporary relevance of those texts for my work as an adult educator. In this, I take up the suggestion of Mary Luke Tobin, SL that Merton was abreast with the feminist movement. At the same time, I take seriously Thomas Merton's involvement with the African American civil rights movement.

More specifically, I opt to bring Merton into dialogue with the Black feminist adult educator and activist, Septima Clark (1898–1987). I found no indications that Thomas Merton and Septima Clark knew each other personally. Merton and Clark were at least linked to each other indirectly by belonging to the same network of civil rights activists. Septima Clark was a friend of Vincent Harding. Thomas Merton was preparing a retreat with Harding. Clark was a colleague of Dorothy F. Cotton within the SCLC.[4] In 1968, Cotton was invited to India to speak with members of a Gandhi organization about the use of nonviolence in the civil rights movement.[5] Merton was at the same time in India, and he had the chance to speak briefly with Cotton in Madras.[6]

Merton has a lot in common with the Black feminist adult educator and activist Septima Clark. Both are sensitive to power relationships and privileges. That is why their approach to education is different from someone like John Dewey. Both are committed to build a worldwide community with like-minded people. In that regard, they both differ from Saul Alinsky who is very skeptical about the possibility of building a community across borders.

---

3. hooks, *Outlaw Culture*, 297.
4. SCLC: Southern Christian Leadership Conference.
5. Cotton, *If Your Back's Not Bent*, 286.
6. Merton and Hart, "Correspondence," 75–76,

THE FIRST ESSAY: LEARNING TO LIVE

In the first essay,[7] Merton describes his view on formation and education in the university, the cloister and outside of it. The prominent themes discussed are: the true and the false self, person versus individual, the relationship between solitude and inter-subjectivity, the superiority of experiences with respect to concepts and abstractions, and a dialogue that is contained in an everyday act.[8]

In delineating contemporary concepts on formation and education, it is relevant to compare Merton's perspective with that of other education authors. A thinker who again is getting full attention today is John Dewey. Although back then, Dewey was already retired for some time, he still was a much-talked-about figure during the years Merton studied at Columbia. In his autobiography, Merton writes quite ironically about him:

> Poor Columbia! It was founded by sincere Protestants as a college predominantly religious. The only thing that remains of that is the university motto: *In lumine tuo videbimus lumen—*, one of the deepest and most beautiful lines in the psalms. "In Thy light, we shall see light." It is, precisely, about grace. It is a line that might serve as the foundation stone of all Christian and Scholastic learning, and which simply has nothing whatever to do with the standards of education at modern Columbia. It might profitably be changed to, *In lumine Randall videbimus Dewey.*[9]

Another option could be to bring Thomas Merton into conversation with the community organizer, Saul Alinsky. In fact, it was Jacques Maritain who urged Merton to get to know this adult educator. Maritain believed that Merton and Alinsky shared "un amour des hommes vraiment évangélique."[10] For Merton though,

---

7. Merton, "Learning to Live." Also published in Merton, *Love and Living,* 3–14.

8. O'Connell, Review of *Merton and Education,* 285.

9. Merton, *Seven Storey Mountain,* 177.

10. "A real evangelical love for humankind." Maritain wrote this letter to Merton in France (Toulouse) on October 23, 1965. I discovered this letter in

Open to the Full Dimension

it was not so clear that he and Alinsky, and for that matter Maritain too, were on the same page. In a letter to Dom Helder Camara, commenting on Maritain's latest book, he writes:

> As for Maritain's book [*Le Paysan de la Garonne*, 1966], yes, I will speak to him about it. His criticism bears, above all, I believe, on philosophy not on politics, since he continues to be in agreement with his radical friends, such as Saul Alinsky.[11]

It seems a better option to look at education authors who regularly refer to Thomas Merton. One author who comes to the fore is the Black feminist author and activist, bell hooks:

> I have been most interested in the mystical dimension of religious experience. And that concern has not been experienced as being in conflict with political concerns, but more as in harmony with them. They are integrated for me, part of a whole. Lately I've been reading Thomas Merton, especially his writings on monastic life, and I can see deep connections between spirituality, the religious experience, and longing to make a space for critical thinking, for contemplation.[12]

During one of the retreats for prioresses of contemplative orders, Merton made a comparison between Martin Luther King Jr. and Malcolm X:

> Malcolm X discovered a world community, he chose his own community. That's a very important thing. After that, he went around to many African States, meeting new brothers and sisters. Earlier, he had spent a long time working in Roxbury. Had he not been killed, he would have become a great man. . . . Martin Luther King Jr., too, is a hero for everybody. But he was much more involved with the establishment. He was a wonderfully

---

2018, while I was doing research in The Thomas Merton Center at Bellarmine University.

11. Merton, *Hidden Ground of Love*, 111.

12. hooks, *Yearning*, 218–19.

good man who had to deal with the political aspect of the machine and sometimes got caught in it.[13]

It is remarkable how Merton introduces here an argument that is also used by authors who have undertaken a feminist analysis of the African American civil rights movement. Through his public actions and his lobbying, Martin Luther King Jr. wanted to maintain good relations with the political establishment. By doing so, he underestimated the leadership taken up by African American women within the civil rights movement.

One of those visionary women was Septima Clark. With her schools for citizenship, she worked to ensure that hundreds of marginalized African American citizens were able to vote. For her, it was important that they felt connected to the civil rights movement even after the public actions. Her education had a strong participative character and focused consistently on local and shared leadership. She said the following about her place within the SCLC:[14]

> Many states are losing their citizenship schools because there is no one to do the follow-up work. I have done as much as I could. In fact, I'm the only paid staff worker doing field visitation. I think that the staff of the SCLC working with me in the Citizenship Education Program feels that the work is not dramatic enough to warrant their time. Direct action is so glamorous and packed with emotion that most young people prefer demonstration over genuine education. Its seems to me as if Citizenship Education is all mine except when it comes time to pick up the checks.[15]

Although Merton saw the importance of the protest actions of the Black civil rights movement, he was convinced it would not suffice to call the culture of racism in the United States to a halt.

---

13. Merton, *Springs of Contemplation*, 86–87.
14. From 1961 onwards, Septima Clark was organizing Citizenship Education for the SCLC.
15. Quoted in McFadden, "Septima P. Clark and the Struggle," 94.

He agreed with Septima Clark that adult education and consciousness-raising were crucial, too.

THE SECOND ESSAY: APOLOGIES TO A NONBELIEVER

It is known of Merton that he immersed himself for years in different faith traditions. He did so by means of study and by encountering representatives of those traditions and maintaining a regular correspondence with them. His personal encounters with the Dalai Lama, Thích Nhất Hạnh, Abraham Heschel, and Daisetz T. Suzuki can be called historical. Less known, but thereby no less important, is his exchange of letters with the Pakistani Sufi Abdul Aziz. He likewise maintained good contacts with atheists, among whom was Erich Fromm.

As a second text, I chose an article that Merton published in *Harper's Magazine*.[16] Here, he reflects on his relationship with non-believers. To clarify the unique character of his approach, it is meaningful to compare it with that of the Highlander Folk School. This school played an important role in the expansion of the African American civil rights movement. Rosa Parks and Martin Luther King Jr. were guests there. Highlander had a secular character but also stood open to diverse religious worldviews. Septima Clark, who was active professionally there since 1955, describes the characteristic trait of this school as follows:

> Highlander had always believed in people and the people trusted its judgement and accepted its leadership. It was accepted by Negroes and whites of all religious faiths because it had always accepted them and made them feel at home. The staff at Highlander knew that the great need of the south was to develop more people to take leadership and responsibility for the causes in which they believed. It set out on a program designed to bring out leadership qualities in people from all walks of life.

16. Merton, "How It Is." Also published in Merton, *Faith and Violence*, 205–14.

Adults from all over the south, about forty at a time, went there for the specific purpose of discussing their problems. They lived together in rustic, pleasant, rural surroundings on the top of the Cumberland plateau in a number of simple cabins around a lake, remote from business and other affairs that normally demand so much attention and energy. Though of different races and often of greatly contrasting economic or educational backgrounds, they rarely felt the tension that such diifferences can cause and if they did, as it occured sometimes, it was never for long. They soon became conscious of the irrelevance of all such differences. Each person talked with people from communities with problems similar to those of his own. Each discussed both formally and informally the successes and difficulties he had had in his efforts to solve these problems in various ways.[17]

Merton shared the same interests of the people at Highlander in order to dialogue across borders of race, faith conviction, class, educational and professional backgrounds. The view of Highlander on education dovetailed strongly with his own monastic perspective:

What people seek today is not so much the organized, predigested routine of conferences and exercises, but an opportunity to be quiet, to reflect, and to discuss in informal, spontaneous and friendly encounters the things they have on their minds. At this point we might add that there is today a far greater interest in contemplation among non-Christians and even nonbelievers than there is among the ordinary run of Christians. Contemplative communities may find that they have a great deal to say to these people who seek spiritual insight but who, generally speaking, are bored to death with preachers and utterly deaf to Christian apologetics. The only Christian communities that still retain some meaning for these people are contemplative communities.[18]

17. Clark, "Literacy and Liberation," 114.
18. Merton, *Contemplation in a World*, 139–40.

Open to the Full Dimension

More than customarily seemed the case in Highlander, Merton emphasized that it was important to take the diversity of worldviews into account because of the unique character of the other and the deepening of dialogue. After the publication of his article in *Harper's Magazine*, he received a letter from Katharina Champney on November 7, 1966. This young woman expressed her distrust towards the institutional church and posed a question to Merton whether he truly was capable of taking her struggle with unbelief seriously. Merton responded to her and afterwards reflected on it in his diary.[19] He formulated ten points of interest that he wanted to take into account in his conversation with this woman. Since, as a Christian he himself was familiar with isolation, doubt, and emptiness, he succeeded in sharing with her the subtle differences in life-convictions:

> Now, you will be irritated with me and think I have got away with the dirty trick I have promised I would not play: that I have insidiously robbed you of your unbelief. That I have elevated you in spite of yourself to the cozy level of the believers. No, I have not. You are an unbeliever. The only thing is that I am also: but in a different way.[20]

Also for Septima Clark it was important to express herself as a believer. Her maturity as a believer helped her to connect secular themes like human rights and religious themes like the role of the Biblical prophets with each other in a nuanced and enriching manner.

THE THIRD ESSAY: THE CONTEMPLATIVE LIFE IN THE MODERN WORLD

In the last text I chose, we arrive at the most familiar aspect of Merton, that of spiritual author. An earlier version of this text appeared in 1965 as an introduction to a Japanese edition of *Seeds of*

---

19. Merton, *Learning to Love*, 158–59.
20. Merton, *Witness to Freedom*, 328.

Contemplation.[21] Merton describes in this essay, in an experiential manner, what he understands by contemplation.

Within the African American civil rights movement, it was not uncommon to share religious experiences with one another. In the course of her life, Septima Clark did so more often. In one of her texts, she gives the following testimony:

> Then my own religious experiences have given me insights into the reality of God that would have been unattainable otherwise.... I have acted on that belief when crushed by disappointments and have lived to see what I thought to be a failure work for the good in my life. I continue to act upon that faith in meeting crises and in determining modes of conduct in life situations. I believe that as long as I do, many of these acts will result in religious experiences that will give me an ever growing reservoir of reasons for believing there is a God. (Senator Leroy Johnson)[22] (James Meredith) (Harvey Gantt).
>
> I believe because I feel it within, because the wonder of the world about me persuades me, because the Bible and human history reveal Him to me, and because my personal experience cause me to say with the apostle Paul "I know Whom I have believed. He is able to keep me until this day."[23]

Thomas Merton declares that contemplation is for everyone, not only for members of religious orders. In a similar manner as Septima Clark, he is convinced that the active life can go hand in hand with deep religious experiences.

> The experience of living faith, the "sense of the presence of God" which many faithful Christians enjoy without being mystics, is a supernatural intuition of God's loving presence and care, granted with the gift of a mature faith.[24]

21. Merton, *Honorable Reader*, 81–92. Also included in Merton, *Faith and Violence*, 215–24.

22. Johnson, 1st State Senator in Georgia since 1870. First Negro in Georgia Legislature since 1907 (footnote in the manuscript, written by Septima Clark).

23. Clark, "Why I Believe," 4.

24. Johnston, *Mysticism of the Cloud*, viii.

Open to the Full Dimension

At the same time, he is aware that life in a contemplative order is linked to a specific vocation. He brought up the uniqueness of this vocation during one of the retreats he conducted for prioresses of contemplative orders:

> The prophetic vocation to which we are called as religious involves a deep awareness of the contradictions in society. We have to feel this keenly. Otherwise, our vocation is going to be watered down or we are going to miss its point. Being called out of the world is not a matter of skipping movies because they're no good or giving up dancing because it's frivolous. We're called to religious life because otherwise we're not free to act from our deepest center, to follow the deepest needs of our life.[25]

CONCLUSION

In this chapter, I have taken three texts as starting points to bring Thomas Merton and Septima Clark into dialogue. I have discovered how the Black feminist approach of Septima Clark and the contemplative perspective of Thomas Merton dovetail strongly with each other.

Both were strongly connected to the African American civil rights movement. Both stressed, it is not enough to protest to achieve equality and social justice. What is needed is a deeper transformation of individuals, communities and societies. Both lived their commitments from a religious and a global perspective, and stressed the importance of adult education and the development of a worldwide community with like-minded people.

Septima Clark and Thomas Merton point out that adult education takes place in a specific social context. If I, as an adult educator in a specific socio-cultural setting, want to do more than merely maintain the social status quo, then it is important that I take into account the diverse power relationships and privileges

---

25. Merton, *Springs of Contemplation*, 147–48.

that exist on different levels in society and that I position myself consciously within them.

Septima Clark and Thomas Merton both discern the difference between a secular and a religious perspective. They invite me to take this difference seriously, even though I find myself often in a context where the secular perspective is dominant. Merton especially reminds me that, only in that way, the dialogue between people with different worldviews can become deeper.

Septima Clark and Thomas Merton are personally convinced that people who are living an active life can arrive at religious experiences. This is possible when one relates to society out of one's own vocation. Both encourage me to preserve an openness to religious experiences in my work.

During the final decade of his life, Merton engaged in an intense dialogue with society. He experienced within his deepest center the many contradictions and injustices that mark our world. He kept close bonds of friendship with men and women around the world. Throughout her life, Septima Clark devoted herself to people at the margins. It would have been wonderful if Septima Clark and Thomas Merton had met each other. Their worldviews and faith experiences were broadened and became deeper throughout their rich lives. The wealth of their multifaceted work remains exceptionally inspiring to this day.

6

Thomas Merton and the Education of Social Justice Allies

TOGETHER WITH SOME OF his trusted friends, Thomas Merton organized in November 1964 a retreat for peace activists: "Spiritual Roots of Protest."[1] One of the central questions he asked was: "*By what right*" do we protest? Merton scholar Gordon Oyer wrote an excellent book about this retreat.[2]

The people who gathered in Gethsemani were experienced peace activists. They were used to focusing on intrapersonal, interpersonal and systemic change. The retreat was under consideration for over two years. During this long preparation process, the organizers became convinced that protest actions should not be the central focus of the retreat, but rather "Spiritual roots of protest." It was the intention of Merton to bring in leaders from different Christian traditions so they could open themselves to, and stimulate each other, in reflecting on these roots.[3]

1. Merton, *Nonviolent Alternative*, 259–60.
2. Oyer, *Pursuing Spiritual Roots*.
3. Del Prete, *Thomas Merton and Education*, 164–65.

Thomas Merton and the Education of Social Justice Allies

While I was reading Oyer, I asked myself what I could learn from this famous retreat. As a Belgian Catholic educator in health care chaplaincy, I'm interested in the education of Catholic chaplains as social justice allies.[4] In today's context, Catholic chaplains cannot restrict themselves to pastoral care of patients and their relatives, or to religious services. They also must critically relate themselves to their organizational and societal context.[5]

When I train Catholic health care chaplains as social justice allies, I make use of an educational and community building method that is called "Intergroup Dialogue." Intergroup Dialogue is a face-to-face, interactive, and facilitated learning experience that brings together twelve to eighteen people from two or more social identity groups. Over a sustained period, they explore commonalities and differences, examine the nature and consequences of systems of power and privilege, and find ways to work together to promote justice.[6]

One of the important thinkers for Intergroup Dialogue is bell hooks. A native from Kentucky, hooks is a Black feminist writer, activist, and educator. Despite the clear and obvious differences, hooks and Merton have some important things in common. They are both known and appreciated as writers. Both can be described as "contemplative activists."[7] What is important for Thomas Merton, as it is for bell hooks, is the education of the whole person.[8] In her work, hooks refers to Thomas Merton.

> Lately, I've been reading Thomas Merton, especially his writings on monastic life, and I can see deep connections

---

4. Reason et al., *Developing Social Justice Allies*; Myhre, "Angle of Vision"; Ramsey, "Faculty Colleagues as Allies"; Lootens, "Diversity Management."
5. Pattison, "Dumbing Down the Spirit."
6. Zúñiga et al., *Intergroup Dialogue*.
7. Mario Aguilar describes Merton as a contemplative activist. See Aguilar, *Thomas Merton*.
8. For Merton's vision on education, see Del Prete, *Thomas Merton and Education*. hooks has developed her vison on education in several publications, for example in hooks, *Teaching Critical Thinking*.

Open to the Full Dimension

between spirituality, the religious experience, and longing to make a space for critical thinking, for contemplation.[9]

In what follows, I introduce some basic principles of Intergroup Dialogue.[10] When meaningful, I will also make reference to hooks. I will use the lens of Intergroup Dialogue to reflect on the educational characteristics of the peacemaker retreat. While I'm doing this, I hope to find out what I can learn from this famous retreat.

INTERGROUP DIALOGUE IS ABOUT RELATIONSHIP BUILDING AND THOUGHTFUL ENGAGEMENT ABOUT DIFFICULT ISSUES

Intergroup Dialogue brings together two or more groups of people who share issues or potential issues of conflict. It may bring together Christians, Moslems, Hindus, and Jews, women and men, multiracial/multiethnic people, migrants and indigenous people, or people with different sexual orientation. It can also bring together several subgroups within larger identity groups, such as Catholics and Protestants, or Europeans of many different ethnic backgrounds.

The group should be small, about twelve to eighteen participants to build more trusting relationships, encourage more engaged interaction, provide greater safety and confidentiality, and make better use of the limited time.

The plan for the peacemaker retreat was to gather male leaders from different Christian traditions. They could stay for a few days in the abbey. Because of logistic reasons, it was not possible at the time to invite female leaders, too. A few years later, Merton did host two retreats for religious women. Those retreats took place in December 1967 and in May 1968. Among other topics, Merton talked about contemplative life as a prophetic vocation.[11] In the Afterword to Oyer's book, John Dear reminds us that Merton also

---

9. hooks, *Yearning*, 219.
10. Schoem and Hurtado, *Intergroup Dialogue*.
11. Merton, *Springs of Contemplation*.

intended to host Martin Luther King Jr., Vincent Harding, and Thích Nhất Hạnh for a retreat in April 1968.[12] It would have been quite an experience from which we also could have learned a lot. During the preparation of the peacemaker retreat, Merton had the intuition that the group should not be too big. He wanted it to be around ten participants. In the end, it turned out to be fourteen participants, Merton included. Members of Catholic (lay and clergy), mainline Protestant, historic peace church, and Unitarian traditions participated. Merton wanted to create an atmosphere in which existential learning could take place.[13]

INTERGROUP DIALOGUE REQUIRES AN EXTENDED COMMITMENT

Intergroup Dialogue is more likely to be meaningful and successful when participants agree to participate for more than a few meetings. With commitment, people realize that they can confront tough issues and know the conversation will continue and move forward at the following meetings.

According to Oyer, not long after the retreat, several participants collaborated in planning a convocation.[14] This illustrates that they were in for a long-term commitment. They invited Merton to write down some reflections that could be read at the end of the program, but in the end that was not possible. This convocation could be viewed as a reprise of some of the issues they engaged at Gethsemani.

---

12. See Oyer, *Pursuing Spiritual Roots*, 234.
13. Merton, *Love and Living*, 3–14.
14. Oyer, *Pursuing Spiritual Roots*, 179–80.

Open to the Full Dimension

INTERGROUP DIALOGUE MAY FOCUS ON RELIGION AND TRADITION, BUT IT CAN ALSO ADDRESS MULTIPLE ISSUES OF SOCIAL IDENTITY THAT EXTEND BEYOND RELIGION AND TRADITION

Because there are so many forces that constitute our individual identity and self, participants may bring in issues of race, gender, class, sexual orientation, and religion at some point in the dialogue.

hooks writes: "I have been most interested in the mystical dimension of religious experience. And that concern has not been experienced as being in conflict with political concerns, but more as in harmony with them."[15]

Intergroup Dialogue that focuses exclusively on the individual processes ignores social structural conditions of power and place in society. On the other hand, Intergroup Dialogue that ignores participant's individual life stories by insisting upon group and/or subgroup identities, denies the unique character of people's lives and diminishes opportunities for personal growth and change.

The starting point of the peacemaker retreat was the religious and spiritual background of the participants. Merton wanted to talk with them about their own religious experiences and beliefs. The participants discussed the spiritual roots of protest on different levels: personal, community and societal. During their conversation, they also discussed issues of privilege, marginality, race, and class.

INTERGROUP DIALOGUE FOCUSES ON BOTH COMMUNITY BUILDING AND INTERGROUP CONFLICT

When people come together in Intergroup Dialogue, they must first overcome their history of keeping apart from others. They need to quickly confront the barriers that divide them, including

---

15. hooks, *Yearning*, 218–19.

the lack of awareness, skills, and knowledge. None of this is easy. At the same time, as people realize how much progress they can make during the gathering, the hard work feels good and the relationships that develop can be heartwarming and enduring.

hooks writes: "Again and again I witnessed a communication breakdown in classroom settings when individuals who were speaking found not only that they had sharp differences of perspective but that attempting to engage in dialogue across these differences aroused intense passions, including anger and sadness. . . . The pressure to maintain a non-combative atmosphere, however, one in which everyone can feel safe, can actually work to silence discussion and/or completely eradicate the possibility of dialectical exchange."[16]

Oyer mentions in his book two moments of conflict: the Mass and the drinking of alcohol during their free time. Merton had some concern about the Mass. He knew that his abbot did not want the Protestants to participate in the Eucharist. Daniel Berrigan, one of the participants who officiated at the Mass, agreed to limit distribution of elements to Catholics. In the end though, all participants received both elements. On the last morning of the retreat, Mennonite John Howard Yoder shared a homily during the Mass.

Oyer writes: "The real conflict was between the abbot *external* to the group and Daniel Berrigan, who felt strongly that Protestants should be included in the Eucharist—not so much conflict *within* the group. Merton was caught in the middle as the "voice" of the abbot, though he personally deferred to Berrigan's decision and supported a Protestant homily. To my knowledge, no one in the group openly opposed including Protestants from their own objection, independently of concern over complying with the abbot's statement."[17]

At the end of the first day, some of the Catholics decided to have a beer. That was not much appreciated by some of the Protestants.

16. hooks, *Teaching Critical Thinking*, 86.
17. April 4, 2015, email to author.

Open to the Full Dimension

In the Afterword to Oyer's book, Dear asks what would have happened if female activists also had participated in the retreat.[18] One could wonder how different the peacemaker retreat could have been if activists from other religious and racial backgrounds had participated. One could imagine that different conflicts or "hot topics" would have come up during the retreat sessions.[19] Black feminist activist hooks stresses the importance of letting anger, sadness and conflict surface in diverse classrooms.[20] If this had happened during the retreat sessions, the participants would have had the opportunity to reflect more deeply on their history of distance, separation, and power imbalance.

INTERGROUP DIALOGUE TAKES PLACE IN AN ATMOSPHERE OF CONFIDENTIALITY

Precisely because Intergroup Dialogue is about relationship building, it requires confidence that what people say during the dialogue will not be reported to nonparticipants. In Intergroup Dialogue, listening is essential and having the opportunity during the program to say words from both the heart and the mind is paramount.

Oyer writes: "I think the biggest need for confidentiality in the Gethsemani setting had to do with protecting from that "hostile element" of the abbot's scrutiny/disapproval. Further, his abbot did not want Merton to take too much of a leadership role—it needed to be an informal conversation. And, Merton was under censure from publically writing on peace and war, so one outcome was that any his comments on the topic should not be published afterward. I didn't sense a need for confidentiality about *most* things they shared—it was after all about protest, which is a very public activity—but all those factors I mentioned called for a certain amount of "confidentiality" among the participants regarding certain matters. I think the fact that Merton chose *not* to share

---

18. Oyer, *Pursuing Spiritual Roots*, 234.
19. Zúñiga et al., *Intergroup Dialogue*, 28.
20. hooks, *Teaching Critical Thinking*, 86.

with novices that Protestants participated in the Eucharist showed he honored the confidentiality of the shared Eucharist."[21]

CONCLUSION

I'm amazed about how easy it is to connect some of the principles of Intergroup Dialogue with the educational characteristics of the peacemaker retreat. Merton wanted to learn from other Christian peace activists. Therefore, he chose to organize this retreat with representatives from different Christian traditions. He took the experience of the participants seriously and invited them to listen and learn from each other.

The retreat was organized for experienced peace activists. It was almost natural for them to have their own practice in the background of the conversation. The retreat most likely inspired them to keep on doing their activist work. In my work as an educator of aspirant social justice allies, I have to think about how to bring in concrete practice. Also, the screening process and the issues of sponsorship need my attention. How to involve facilitators from different social identity backgrounds is also an important question for me. Because of the working context of Belgian Catholic health care chaplains, it is crucial to create an atmosphere of confidentiality.

The uniqueness of the retreat was not to put concrete protest strategies at the center of the conversation. Making "Spiritual Roots of Protest" the central topic can be linked with Merton's view on education.

> The fruit of education, whether in the university . . . or in the monastery . . . was the activation of the inmost center, . . . which is a freedom beyond freedom, a self beyond all ego, a being beyond the created realm, an identity beyond essence, and a consciousness that transcends all division, all separation.[22]

---

21. April 4, 2015, email to author.
22. Merton, *Love and Living*, 9.

Open to the Full Dimension

This contemplative view was based on his long experience as a monk and pastoral practitioner, particularly as a master of scholastics, master of novices, spiritual director, organizer of retreats, lecturer, scholar, author, artist, and letter writer. Merton learned over the years that it was his vocation to be open to the full dimension.

> Without experienced guides who are completely open to the full dimension—the mystical and prophetic dimension—of love in Christ, renewal will mean little more than the replacement of old rules by new ones and of old traditions by novel frenzies.[23]

Thomas Merton has been an experienced guide who has helped me to view my own vocation as a pastoral supervisor and educator from a contemplative and prophetic perspective. I believe that his voice will accompany me through my life and professional practice in the years to come.

---

23. Merton, *Contemplation in a World*, 25.

Appendix

Letter of Thomas Merton to Cardinal Suenens

jhs
Sept. 10, 1964
To His Eminence Cardinal Suenens
Rome.

I take this opportunity to say a few words about the disputed question of the apostolate of monks who are living in the cloister. The fact that a good friend and neighbor is planning to consult with you at the Council gives me this occasion.

Permit me to say in all simplicity that I feel that I am in a position to say something on this subject as I am a member of the cloistered Cistercian Order of the Strict Observance, and I have been for about twenty-three years. During this time, the writing of books and ecumenical contacts with retreatants at the monastery have afforded me opportunities and experiences in a "monastic apostolate." It seems to me that the following points might be noted:

Appendix

The cloistered and contemplative monastery has a very important part to play in the apostolate of the Church today. But the efficacy of the monastic apostolate depends first of all on the authenticity of the monastic life. The silent and contemplative life of the monk exercises a certain appeal on modern man even though they might feel hostile or ambivalent towards it. He recognizes correctly that the monk, by his life of silent prayer, labor, study, and solitude, is affirming the existence and reality of transcendent spiritual values which are not to be found in a life of unregulated activism, and which are necessary to some extent even for a happy and fruitful life of ordered action in the world. Thus the monk contributes something irreplaceable to the world, simply by being a monk. This is his first obligation.

The monastic apostolate will then necessarily be the apostolate of contemplatives, and not an organized and systematic life of action for the ordinary care of souls. To take the monk from his contemplative life and immerse him in routines and techniques for which he has neither understanding nor capacity, would be of no use to the church or to the monk himself. Whereas if the monk is able to live his monastic life fully, there will certainly be an "overflow" which will be of inestimable apostolic value provided that its spontaneity and authenticity are fully protected by the church. The apostolate of the contemplative monk can and should therefore be something quite unique in the church.

The apostolate of the contemplative will normally be limited and specialize. It should normally be an apostolate that can be exercised without leaving the solitude of the cloister, and writing recommends itself in this respect as a form of apostolate wholly compatible with the monastic life, provided that there is evidence that the one called to be a monk also shows clear signs of a vocation to be a writer. There is little benefit to be derived from a merely routine production of "writings" on the part of monks with little or nothing to say. The monk need not write if he only repeats what is said better by someone else.

Where special talents exist, then the monk can also exercise a certain apostolate by works of sacred art and music. The contemplative monastery might also be a center for retreats and conferences of sacred artists and musicians. The monk may often have a vocation to <u>scholarship and research</u> which may directly or indirectly be rich in apostolic fruit.

Naturally, the chief apostolic venture of the cloistered monastery of men will probably be in the realm of <u>retreats and spiritual direction</u>. Normally the contemplative monk may be expected to undertake direction and conferences with the elite of the active apostolate, and his monastery will provide these apostles with a place in which to seek a much needed refreshment of body and spirit in order to gain strength for further efforts in active work.

<u>Education</u> however should not be considered the ordinary province of the contemplative monk, except in very limited and restricted or specialized forms. <u>Parish work</u> should not normally be undertaken by contemplative monks. However monks of contemplative Orders might certainly be encouraged or at least permitted to leave their monastery to preach retreats in other contemplative monasteries or in religious houses, or under other circumstances which would retain an affinity to their own cloistered vocations. In certain very exceptional cases, monks of contemplative Orders might be permitted to teach or lecture outside their monastery, especially in religious houses or colleges. But it must be noted also that in the United States particularly there is reason to believe that members of contemplative Orders might profitably give lectures or conferences even in secular universities and non-Catholic colleges when they are specially invited to do so because of some special competency. In this one area it would seem that the exceptional strictness of the contemplative Orders might be slightly relaxed with greater benefit then if the priests of these Orders were indiscriminately sent out to work in parishes.

In conclusion, the apostolate of contemplative monks, while being primarily an apostolate of prayer and sacrifice, can and may also occasionally be an apostolate of writing, preaching (retreats), sacred art, scholarship, or even teaching in the sense of occasional lecturing. But this apostolate should retain a specialized, limited and unusual character, so that the "charism" of the monastic and

Appendix

contemplative life might above all be respected and the Spirit not extinguished. For it can be said of the contemplative monk more than any other: if the salt shall lose its favor, where shall we go to look for salting?

Bibliography

Aguilar, Mario I. *Thomas Merton: Contemplation and Political Action*. London: SPCK, 2011.
Balthasar, Hans Urs von. *Cosmic Liturgy: The Universe According to Maximus the Confessor*. Translated by Brian E. Daley, SJ. San Francisco: Ignatius, 2003.
———. *Liturgie Cosmique: Maxime le Confesseur*. Translated by L. Lhaumet and H.-A. Prentout. Paris: Aubier, 1947.
Behr-Sigel, Elisabeth. "Hesychasm and the Western Impact in Russia: St. Tikhon of Zandonsk (1724-1783)." In *Christian Spirituality: Post-Reformation and Modern*, edited by Louis Dupré and Don E. Saliers, in collaboration with John Meyendorff, 432-46. New York: Crossroad, 1989.
———. "The Meaning of Ministry." In *Orthodox Women Speak: Discerning the Signs of the Times*, edited by Kyriaki Karidoyanes FitzGerald, 93-97. Geneva: WCC, 1999.
———. *The Place of the Heart: An Introduction to Orthodox Spirituality*. Torrance, CA: Oakwood, 1992.
Bielawski, Maciej. "Merton's Margin." In *Studia Mertoniana 2*, edited by Krzysztof Bielawski, 81-88. Krakow: Homini, 2003.
Blowers, Paul M. *Exegesis and Spiritual Pedagogy in Maximus the Confessor: An Investigation of the Quaestiones ad Thalassium*. Notre Dame, IN: University of Notre Dame Press, 1991.
Carr, Anne C. *A Search for Wisdom & Spirit: Thomas Merton's Theology of the Self*. Notre Dame, IN: University of Notre Dame Press, 1988.
Clark, Septima P. "Literacy and Liberation." *Freedomways* 4 (1964) 113-24.

Bibliography

———. "Why I Believe There Is a God." Septima P. Clark Papers, Avery Research Center, College of Charleston. https://lcdl.library.cofc.edu/lcdl/catalog/lcdl:92642.

Clayton, Mark P. "Contemplative Chaplaincy? A View from a Children's Hospice." *Practical Theology* 6 (2013) 35–50.

———. "A Hidden Wholeness: Spiritual Care in a Children's Hospice." In *Critical Care. Delivering Spiritual Care in Healthcare Contexts*, edited by Jonathan Pye et al., 249–60. Philadelphia: Jessica Kingsley, 2015.

Cotton, Dorothy F. *If Your Back's Not Bent. The Role of the Citizenship Education Program in the Civil Rights Movement*. New York: Atria, 2012.

Creaner, Mary. "Reflections on Learning and Transformation in Supervision: A Crucible of My Experience." In *Supervision as Transformation: A Passion for Learning*, edited by Robin Shohet, 146–59. London: Jessica Kingsley, 2011.

Cunningham, Lawrence S. *Thomas Merton and the Monastic Vision*. Grand Rapids: Eerdmans, 1999.

Del Prete, Thomas. *Thomas Merton and the Education of the Whole Person*. Birmingham, AL: Religious Education Press, 1990.

Dillen, Annemie, et al. "Wat Doe Jij hier Eigenlijk? Resultaten van Empirisch Onderzoek naar de Tijdsbesteding van Vlaamse Ziekenhuispastores." *Collationes* 48 (2018) 163–90.

Elliott, John H. *A Home for the Homeless: A Social-Scientific Criticism of 1 Peter, Its Situation and Strategy*. Eugene, OR: Wipf & Stock, 2005.

Fekete, Liz. *A Suitable Enemy: Racism, Migration and Islamophobia in Europe*. New York: Pluto, 2009.

Ferrant, Vincent. "Vier Weken voor een Ziekenhuispastor." In *God in Heel de Schepping: Jonge Jezuïeten over de Inspiratie van Ignatius van Loyola*, edited by Rob Faesen et al.,146–53. Kapellen: DNB/Pelckmans, 1990.

Fitzgerald, Elisabeth M., et al. "Nurses Need Not Be Guilty Bystanders: Caring for Vulnerable Immigrant Populations." *The Online Journal of Issues in Nursing* 22 (2016) 1–11. https://ojin.nursingworld.org/MainMenuCategories/ANAMarketplace/ANAPeriodicals/OJIN/TableofContents/Vol-22-2017/No1-Jan-2017/Articles-Previous-Topics/Nurses-Need-Not-Be-Guilty-Bystanders.html.

Foltz, Bruce V. *The Noetics of Nature: Environmental Philosophy and the Holy Beauty of the Visible*. New York: Fordham University Press, 2014.

Graham, Elaine, et al., eds. *Theological Reflection: Methods*. London: SCM, 2005.

———. *Theological Reflection: Sources*. London: SCM, 2007.

Hall, Cassidy. Review of *Thomas Merton for Our Time* (12 Lectures on 4 CDs), by Daniel P. Horan, OFM. *The Merton Seasonal* 43 (2018) 28–31.

Haynes, Jeffrey. "Constructions of European Identity in Relation to the Muslim Other During the Age of Globalization." In *Perceptions of Islam in Europe: Culture, Identity, and the Muslim Other*, edited by Hakan Yilmaz and Çağla E. Aykaç, 49–69. London: I. B. Tauris, 2012.

Hiuser, Kris. *Animals, Theology and the Incarnation*. London: SCM, 2017.

Bibliography

Holder, Arthur. "The Problem with Spiritual Classics." *Spiritus* 10 (2010) 22–37.

hooks, bell. *Outlaw Culture*. New York: Routledge, 1994.

———. *Teaching Critical Thinking: Practical Wisdom*. New York: Routledge, 2010.

———. *Yearning: Race, Gender, and Cultural Politics*. Boston: South End, 1991.

Horan, Daniel P. *Thomas Merton for Our Time* (12 lectures on 4 CDs). Rockville, MD: Now You Know Media, 2017.

Inchausti, Robert. *Thinking through Thomas Merton: Contemplation for Contemporary Times*. Albany, NY: State University of New York Press, 2014.

Johnston, William. *The Mysticism of the Cloud of Unknowing*. Foreword by Thomas Merton. Wheathampstead, UK: Anthony Clarke, 1987.

Karras, Valerie A. "Patristic Gender Anthropology in Behr-Sigel." In *A Communion in Faith and Love: Elisabeth Behr-Sigel's Ecclesiology*, edited by Sarah Hinlicky Wilson and Aikaterini Pekridou, 68–85. Geneva: World Council of Churches, 2017.

Kehoe, Deborah. "Thomas Merton's Ecopoetry: Bearing Witness to the Unity of Creation." *The Merton Annual* 22 (2009) 170–88.

Kern, Archimandrite Cyprien. "Les Eléments de la Théologie de Grégoire Palamas." *Irénikon* 20 (1947) 6–33; 164–93.

Kern, Archimandrite Kyprian. *Orthodox Pastoral Service*. St. Paul, MN: OCABS, 2018.

Kern, Cyprian. "Two Models of the Pastorate." In *Tradition Alive: On the Church and the Christian Life in Our Time*, edited by Michael Plekon, 107–20. Lanham, MD: Rowman & Littlefield, 2003.

Kilcourse, George A. *Ace of Freedoms: Thomas Merton's Christ*. Notre Dame, IN: University of Notre Dame Press, 1993.

Kilcourse, George A., and Paul Stokell. "Life through the Lens of Inner and Outer Freedom: An Interview with Jane Marie Richardson, SL." *Thomas Merton Annual* 13 (2000) 127–43.

Kramer, Dewey W., and Victor A. Kramer. "Growing into Responsibility: An Interview with Mary Luke Tobin." *The Merton Annual* 2 (1989) 43–56.

Kwok, Pui-lan. "A Theology of Border Passage." In *Border Crossings: Cross-Cultural Hermeneutics*, edited by Devadasan Nithya Premnath, 103–17. Maryknoll, NY: Orbis, 2007.

Ladouceur, Paul. *Modern Orthodox Theology*. New York: T. & T. Clark, 2019.

Lartey, Emmanuel Y. *Pastoral Theology in an Intercultural World*. Peterborough, UK: Epworth, 2006.

Leach, Jane. "Pastoral Theology as Attention." *Contact* 153 (2007) 19–32.

Leach, Jane, and Michael Paterson. *Pastoral Supervision: A Handbook*. 2nd ed. London: SCM, 2015.

Leach, Jane, and Michael Paterson, in collaboration with Dominiek Lootens. *Pastorale Supervisie: Een Handboek*. Oud-Turnhout: Gompel & Svacina, 2019.

Lemaitre, J. "Contemplation: III. Contemplation chez les Grecs et Autres Orientaux Chrétiens." In *Dictionnaire de Spiritualité* 2, 1787–1872.

Bibliography

Loobuyck, Patrick. *De Seculiere Samenleving. Over Religie, Atheïsme en Democratie.* Antwerpen: Houtekiet, 2013.

Lootens, Dominiek. "Diversity Management in European Healthcare Organizations: The Catholic Chaplain as Advocate." In *Intercultural and Interreligious Pastoral Caregiving: The SIPCC, 1995–2015: 20 Years of International Practice and Reflection*, edited by Karl Federschmidt and Daniel Louw, 201–14. Norderstedt: Books on Demand, 2015.

———. *Die Kraft der Phantasie in Bildungsarbeit und Seelsorge: Lernen von Kierkegaard.* Freiburg: Lambertus, 2009.

———. "Thomas Merton and the Spiritual Roots of Protest: Educational Reflections on the Peacemaker Retreat." *The Merton Seasonal* 42 (2017) 12–16.

———. "Wanneer Men Samen Droomt, Begint een Nieuwe Werkelijkheid: Een Gesprek met Birgit Burbaum." *Pastorale Perspectieven* 152 (2011) 33–38.

Lossky, Olga. *Toward the Endless Day: The Life of Elisabeth Behr-Sigel.* Notre Dame, IN: University of Notre Dame Press, 2010.

Lossky, Vladimir. *The Mystical Theology of the Eastern Church.* London: James Clarke & Co, 1957.

Louth, Andrew. "Between Creation and Transfiguration: The Environment in the Eastern Orthodox Tradition." In *Ecological Hermeneutics: Biblical, Historical and Theological Perspectives*, edited by David G. Horrell et al., 196–210. London: T. & T. Clark, 2010.

———. *Maximus the Confessor.* London: Routledge, 1996.

———. *Wisdom of the Byzantine Church: Evagrius of Pontos and Maximos the Confessor.* Columbia, MO: University of Missouri, 1997.

Marcuse, Herbert. *One-Dimensional Man: Studies in the Ideology of Advanced Industrial Society.* Boston: Beacon, 1966.

Maxime le Confesseur. *Centuries sur la Charité.* Translated by Joseph Pegon, SJ. Paris: Editions du Cerf, 1945.

Maximos the Confessor. *On Difficulties in the Church Fathers: The Ambigua.* Translated by Nicholas Constas. Cambridge, MA: Harvard University Press, 2014.

———. *On Difficulties in Sacred Scripture: The Responses to Thalassios.* Translated by Fr. Maximos Constas. Washington, DC: The Catholic University of America Press, 2018.

Maximus the Confessor. *The Ascetic Life: The Four Centuries of Charity.* Translated by Polycarp Sherwood, OSB. New York: Newman, 1955.

———. *Selected Writings.* Translated by George C. Berthold. New York: Paulist, 1985.

McCaslin, Susan. "Transformative Solitudes: Merton and Rilke and the Pivot of Silence." *The Merton Seasonal* 35 (2010) 15–25.

McCloskey, Elizabeth. "More Than a Footnote: The Footprints of Mary Luke Tobin at Vatican II." *The Merton Seasonal* 32 (2007) 10–32.

McFadden, Grace Jordan. "Septima P. Clark and the Struggle for Human Rights." In *Women in the Civil Rights Movement: Trailblazers & Torchbearers 1941–*

Bibliography

1965, edited by Vicki L. Crawford et al., 85–97. Bloomington: Indiana University Press.

Meade, Mark C. "From Downtown Louisville to Buenos Aires: Victoria Ocampo as Thomas Merton's Overlooked Bridge to Latin America and the World." *The Merton Annual* 26 (2013) 168–80.

Merton, Thomas. *The Asian Journal of Thomas Merton*. Edited by Naomi Burton et al. New York: New Directions, 1973.

———. *Bread in the Wilderness*. New York: New Directions, 1953.

———. *Cassian and the Fathers*. Edited by Patrick F. O'Connell. Kalamazoo, MI: Cistercian, 2005.

———. "Comments about the Religious Life Today: Transcript of a Recording Made by and Edited by Father Louis Merton for Special General Chapter Sisters of Loretto, 1967." *The Merton Annual* 14 (2001) 14–32.

———. *Conjectures of a Guilty Bystander*. Garden City, NY: Doubleday, 1966.

———. *Contemplation in a World of Action*. Garden City, NY: Doubleday, 1971.

———. *Dancing in the Water of Life. Seeking Peace in the Hermitage*. Edited by Robert E. Daggy. San Francisco: HarperSanFrancisco, 1997.

———. *Day of a Stranger*. Edited by Robert E. Daggy. Salt Lake City, UT: Gibbs M. Smith, 1981.

———. *Faith and Violence: Christian Teaching and Christian Practice*. Notre Dame, IN: University of Notre Dame Press.

———. *The Hidden Ground of Love: Letters on Religious Experience and Social Concerns*. Edited by William H. Shannon. New York: Farrar, Straus & Giroux, 1985.

———. *Honorable Reader: Reflections on My Work*. Edited by Robert E. Daggy. New York: Crossroad, 1989.

———. "How It Is: Apologies to an Unbeliever." *Harper's Magazine* 223 (1966) 38–39.

———. *The Inner Experience: Notes on Contemplation*. Edited by William H. Shannon. San Francisco: HarperSanFrancisco, 2003.

———. *An Introduction to Christian Mysticism*. Edited by Patrick F. O'Connell. Kalamazoo, MI: Cistercian, 2008.

———. "Learning to Live." In *University on the Heights*, edited by Wesley First, 187–99. New York: Doubleday, 1969.

———. *Learning to Love. Exploring Solitude and Freedom*. Edited by Christine M. Bochen. San Francisco: HarperSanFrancisco, 1997.

———. *A Life in Letters: The Essential Collection*. Edited by William H. Shannon and Christine M. Bochen. Notre Dame, IN: Ave Maria, 2008.

———. *The Literary Essays of Thomas Merton*. Edited by Patrick Hart, OCSO. New York: New Directions, 1981.

———. *Love and Living*. Edited by Naomi Burton Stone and Patrick Hart, OCSO. New York: Farrar, Straus & Giroux, 1979.

———. *Monastic Peace*. Saint Paul, MN: North Central, 1958.

———. *Mystics & Zen Masters*. New York: Farrar, Straus & Giroux, 1967.

———. *The New Man*. New York: Farrar, Straus & Cudahy, 1961.

———. *New Seeds of Contemplation*. New York: New Directions, 1961.

Bibliography

———. *The Nonviolent Alternative*. Edited by Gordon C. Zahn. New York: Farrar, Straus & Giroux, 1980.

———. *Opening the Bible*. Collegeville, MN: Liturgical, 1986.

———. "Orthodoxy and the World." In *Merton and Hesychasm: The Prayer of the Heart*, edited by Bernadette Dieker and Jonathan Montaldo, 473–84. Louisville, KY: Fons Vitae, 2003.

———. *Passion for Peace: The Social Essays*. Edited by William H. Shannon. New York: Crossroad, 1995.

———. *Raids on the Unspeakable*. New York: New Directions, 1966.

———. "Sanctity in the Epistles of St Paul: Parts VI-VII, 3." *Liturgy O.C.S.O.* 30 (1996) 15–33.

———. *A Search for Solitude: Pursuing the Monk's True Life*. Edited by Lawrence S. Cunningham. San Francisco: HarperSanFrancisco, 1996.

———. *The Seven Storey Mountain*. New York: Harcourt, Brace & Company, 1948.

———. *Spiritual Direction & Meditation*. Collegeville, MN: Liturgical, 1987.

———. *The Springs of Contemplation: A Retreat at the Abbey of Gethsemani*. Edited by Jane Marie Richardson. New York: Farrar, Straus & Giroux, 1992.

———. "Statement on Clerical Celibacy." *The Merton Seasonal* 4 (1979) 8.

———. "St. Maximus the Confessor on Non-Violence." In *Passion for Peace: The Social Essays*, edited by William H. Shannon, 241–47. New York: Crossroad, 1995.

———. *Thoughts in Solitude*. New York: Farrar, Straus & Cudahy, 1958.

———. *A Vow of Conversation: Journals 1964–1965*. Edited by Naomi Burton Stone. New York: Farrar, Straus & Giroux, 1988.

———. *The Wisdom of the Desert*. New York: New Directions, 1960.

———. *Witness to Freedom. Letters in Times of Crisis*. Edited by William H. Shannon. New York: Farrar, Straus & Giroux, 1994.

———. *Zen and the Birds of Appetite*. New York: New Directions, 1968.

Merton, Thomas, and Patrick Hart. "Correspondence (1962–1968)." *The Merton Annual* 32 (2019) 11–77.

Merton, Thomas, and Victoria Ocampo. *Fragmentos de un Regalo: Correspondencia y Artículos y Reseñas Publicados en Sur*. Translated by Juan Javier Negri. Buenos Aires: Sur, 2011.

Miles, Margaret. R. *Practicing Christianity: Critical Perspectives for an Embodied Spirituality*. Eugene, OR: Wipf & Stock, 1988.

———. *Reading for Life: Beauty, Pluralism, and Responsibility*. New York: Continuum, 1997.

———. *Recollections and Reconsiderations*. Eugene, OR: Wipf & Stock, 2018.

Mills, William C. *Church, World, and Kingdom: The Eucharistic Foundation of Alexander Schmemann's Pastoral Theology*. Chicago: Liturgy Training, 2012.

Myhre, Paul. O. "Angle of Vision from a Companion/Ally in Teaching for a Culturally Diverse and Racially Just World." In *Teaching for a Culturally*

Bibliography

Diverse and Racially Just World, edited by Eleazar S. Fernandez, 219–37. Eugene, OR: Cascade, 2014.

Norwood, Frances. "The Ambivalent Chaplain: Negotiating Structural and Ideological Difference on the Margins of Modern-Day Medicine." *Medical Anthropology* 25 (2006) 1–29.

O'Connell, Patrick F. Review of *Thomas Merton and the Education of the Whole Person*, by Thomas Del Prete. *The Merton Annual* 4 (1991) 284–88.

———. Review of *Thomas Merton on Contemplation* (Introduction by Fr. Anthony Ciorra + 5 Lectures: 4 CDs); *Finding True Meaning and Beauty* (4 Lectures: 2 CDs); *Thomas Merton's Great Sermons* (Introduction by Fr. Anthony Ciorra + 4 Lectures: 2 CDs); *Vatican II: The Sacred Liturgy and the Religious Life* (7 Lectures: 4 CDs); *Thomas Merton on Sufism* (Introduction by Fr. Anthony Ciorra + 13 Lectures: 7 CDs); *Ways of Prayer: A Desert Father's Wisdom* (Introduction by Fr. Anthony Ciorra + 13 Lectures: 7 CDs); *Thomas Merton on the 12 Degrees of Humility* (Introduction by Fr. Anthony Ciorra + 16 Lectures: 8 CDs); *Solitude and Togetherness* (Introduction by Fr. Anthony Ciorra + 11 Lectures: 11 CDs); *The Prophet's Freedom* (Introduction by Fr. Anthony Ciorra + 8 Lectures: 8 CDs), by Thomas Merton. *The Merton Annual* 26 (2013) 230–32.

Oyer, Gordon. *Pursuing the Spiritual Roots of Protest: Merton, Berrigan, Yoder, and Muste at the Gethsemani Abbey Peacemaker Retreat*. Foreword by Jim Forest, Afterword by John Dear, SJ. Eugene, OR: Cascade, 2014.

Padovano, Anthony. *A Retreat with Thomas Merton: Becoming Who We Are*. Cincinnati, OR: St. Anthony Messenger, 1995.

Palmer, G. E. H., et al., eds. *The Philokalia: The Complete Text Compiled by St Nikodimus of the Holy Mountain and St Makarios of Corinth*. London: Faber & Faber, 1981.

Palmer, Parker J. *The Active Life: A Spirituality of Work, Creativity, and Caring*. New York: Jossey-Bass, 1990.

———. *The Promise of Paradox. A Celebration of Contradictions in the Christian Life*. New York: Jossey-Bass, 2008.

Paterson, Michael. "From Therapeutic Leftovers to Public Theology." In *Enriching Ministry: Pastoral Supervision in Practice*, edited by Michael Paterson and Jessica Rose, 3–20. London: SCM, 2014.

Pattison, Stephen. "Dumbing Down the Spirit." In *Spirituality in Health Care Contexts*, edited by Helen Orchard, 33–46. London: Jessica Kingsley, 2001.

———. *Shame: Theory, Therapy, Theology*. Cambridge, UK: Cambridge University Press, 2000.

Pearson, Paul M. "A Voice for Racial Justice." *The Merton Seasonal* 40 (2015) 46–47.

Pembroke, Neil. "Merton's True Self and the Psychology of the Dialogical Self." *Religious Studies and Theology* 2 (2007) 191–210.

———. *Moving toward Spiritual Maturity. Psychological, Contemplative, and Moral Challenges in Christian Living*. New York: Routledge, 2007.

Bibliography

———. "Two Spiritualities of Self-Emptying. Weil's Decreation and Merton's Emptying out the False Self." *Studies in Spirituality* 25 (2015) 267–78.

Pędziwiatr, Konrad. *The New Muslim Elites in European Cities: Religion and Active Social Citizenship amongst Young Organized Muslims in Brussels and London.* Saarbrücken: VDM, 2010.

Pew Research Center. "Being Christian in Western Europe." http://www.pewforum.org/2018/05/29/being-christian-in-western-europe/.

———. "Europe's Growing Muslim Population." http://www.pewforum.org/2017/11/29/europes-growing-muslim-population/.

Phan, Peter C. "The Experience of Migration in the US as a Source of Intercultural Theology." In *Migration, Religious Experience, and Globalization*, edited by Gioacchino Campese, CS, and Pietro Ciallella, CS, 143–69. New York: Center for Migration Studies, 2003.

Poks, Małgorzata. "Lamb Admits Ties to Cain—The Human, the Less-Than-Human, and the Kin(g)dom in Thomas Merton's *The Geographie of Lograire*." In *Guard the Human Image for It Is the Image of God: Essays on Thomas Merton*, edited by Gary Hall and Detlev Cuntz, 116–31. Münsterschwarzach: Vier-Türme, 2019.

Polis, Harold. "De Kleur van Zorg. Patrick Loobuyck Zoekt naar Hedendaagse Ethische Waarden." *Weliswaar* 126 (2015) 26–27.

Pramuk, Christopher. *Sophia: The Hidden Christ of Thomas Merton.* Collegeville, MN: Liturgical, 2009.

Ramsey, Nancy. "Faculty Colleagues as Allies in Resisting Racism." In *Teaching for a Culturally Diverse and Racially Just World*, edited by Eleazar S. Fernandez, 238–52. Eugene, OR: Cascade, 2014.

Reason, Robert D., et al., eds. *Developing Social Justice Allies.* San Francisco: Jossey-Bass, 2005.

Rigby, Cynthia L. "Scandalous Presence: Incarnation and Trinity." In *Feminist and Womanist Essays in Reformed Dogmatics*, edited by Amy Plantinga Pauw and Serene Jones, 58–74. Louisville, KY: Westminster John Knox, 2006.

Russell, Norman. *Gregory Palamas and the Making of Palamism in the Modern Age.* Oxford: Oxford University Press, 2019.

Schoem, David, and Sylvia Hurtado, eds. *Intergroup Dialogue: Deliberative Democracy in School, College, Community, and Workplace.* Ann Arbor, MI: University of Michigan Press, 2001.

Serrán-Pagán y Fuentes, Cristóbal, ed. *Merton & the Tao: Dialogues with John Wu and the Ancient Sages.* Louisville, KY: Fons Vitae, 2013.

Sheldrake, Philip. "Contemplation and Social Transformation: The Example of Thomas Merton." *Acta Theologica Supplementum* 11 (2008) 181–97.

———. *Explorations in Spirituality: History, Theology, and Social Practice.* New York: Paulist, 2010.

———. *Spirituality and History: Questions of Interpretation and Method.* Maryknoll, NY: Orbis, 1995.

Bibliography

Snyder, Susanna. *Asylum-Seeking, Migration and Church.* Farnham, UK: Ashgate, 2012.

Thunberg, Lars. *Microcosm and Mediator: The Theological Anthropology of Maximus the Confessor.* Lund: C. W. K. Gleerup, 1965.

———. *Microcosm and Mediator: The Theological Anthropology of Maximus the Confessor.* 2nd ed. Chicago: Open Court, 1995.

Thurston, Bonnie B. "An Absolute Duty to Rebel: Thomas Merton, Religious Women and the Challenges of Vatican II." *The Merton Seasonal* 39 (2014) 14–25.

———. "The Best Retreat I Ever Made: Merton and the Contemplative Prioresses." *The Merton Annual* 14 (2001) 81–95.

———. "Islam in Alaska: Sufi Material in Thomas Merton in Alaska." *The Merton Seasonal* 29 (2004) 3–8.

Thurston, Bonnie, and Mary Swain, eds. *Hidden in the Same Mystery: Thomas Merton and Loretto.* Louisville, KY: Fons Vitae, 2010.

Tollefsen, Torstein T. *The Christocentric Cosmology of St Maximus the Confessor.* Oxford: Oxford University Press, 2008.

Tracy, David. "A Correlational Model of Practical Theology Revisited." In *Invitation to Practical Theology: Catholic Voices and Visions*, edited by Claire Wolfteich, 70–86. New York: Paulist, 2014.

———. "Recent Catholic Spirituality: Unity amid Diversity." In *Christian Spirituality: Post-Reformation and Modern*, edited by Louis Dupré and Don E. Saliers, in collaboration with John Meyendorff, 143–73. New York: Crossroad, 1989.

Trible, Phyllis. *God and Rhetoric of Sexuality.* London: SCM, 1978.

Valliere, Paul. *Modern Russian Theology: Bukharev, Soloviev. Bulgakov: Orthodox Theology in a New Key.* Grand Rapids, Eerdmans, 2000.

Van Lierde, Emmanuel. "Verschil Scherp Stellen om Eigenheid te Bewaren: Jezuïet Vincent Ferrant over Interlevensbeschouwelijk Samenwerken in Ziekenhuizen." In *Ontsluitende Zorg: De Toekomst van het Pastorale Beroep*, edited by Dominiek Lootens, 60–67. Antwerpen: Halewijn/UCSIA, 2011.

Veling, Terry A. *Practical Theology: On Earth as It Is in Heaven.* Maryknoll, NY: Orbis, 2005.

Waldron, Robert. *Thomas Merton: Master of Attention.* New York: Paulist, 2008.

Weaver, Mary J. "Conjectures of a Disenchanted Reader." *Horizons* 30 (2003) 285–96.

Weis, Monica. *The Environmental Vision of Thomas Merton.* Lexington, KY: The University Press of Kentucky, 2011.

———. "Ishi Means Man: Book Reviews that Critique Society." *The Merton Seasonal* 24 (1999) 9–13.

———. "Merton's Fascination with Deer: A Graceful Symphony." *The Merton Journal* 15 (2008) 33–46.

———. "The Prophetic Merton—Once Again." *The Merton Seasonal* 36 (2011) 11–16.

Bibliography

———. *Thomas Merton and the Celts: A New World Opening Up.* Eugene, OR: Pickwick, 2016.

Weld, Nicki. *A Practical Guide to Transformative Supervision for the Helping Professions: Amplifying Insight.* London: Jessica Kingsley, 2012.

Williams, Rowan. *A Silent Action: Engagements with Thomas Merton.* London: SPCK, 2013.

Wilson, Sarah Hinlicky. *Woman, Women, and the Priesthood in the Trinitarian Theology of Elisabeth Behr-Sigel.* London: Bloomsbury, 2013.

Wolfteich, Claire. "Animating Questions: Spirituality and Practical Theology." *International Journal of Practical Theology* 13 (2009) 121–43.

———. "Practices of Unsaying: Michel de Certeau, Spirituality Studies, and Practical Theology." *Spiritus* 12 (2012) 161–71.

———. "Spirituality." In *The Wiley Blackwell Companion to Practical Theology*, edited by Bonnie J. Miller-McLemore, 328–36. Chichester, UK: Wiley-Blackwell, 2012.

Zúñiga, Ximena, et al. *Intergroup Dialogue in Higher Education: Meaningful Learning About Social Justice.* New York: Wiley, 2011.

Index

adult education, ix, 76–87
Alinsky, Saul, 78–80
Allchin, Donald, 57
animal theology, 53, 55–57, 74
artists, xx, 1, 9, 96, 99
The Asian Journal (Merton), xxvi
attention, xxvi, 25, 31, 41, 46–47,
    51–52, 76, 79, 83, 95
Australia, xxi–xxii
Aziz, Abdul, 24–25, 27, 46, 54, 63,
    74, 82

Balthasar, Hans Urs von, 57–59, 71
Behr-Sigel, Elisabeth, xxvii, 54,
    70–75
Belgium, xiv, xix–xx, xxvi, 3–9, 14,
    67, 89, 95
Berrigan, Daniel, 2, 93
Bible, xviii, xx, 3, 18, 22–23, 32, 37,
    41, 48, 50–51, 55, 57–59, 62,
    65, 68, 71–75, 85
body, 54, 64–65, 74, 99
Bread in the Wilderness (Merton), 60
Bulgakov, Sergius, 66, 70

Bultmann, Rudolf, 49

Camara, Dom Helder, 2, 80
Cardenal, Ernesto, 2
Cardinal Suenens, xiv, xix–xx,
    97–100
Carr, Anne E., xxiv
Catholic, xviii, xxiii, xxvi–xxvii,
    1–16, 20, 33, 71–72, 89–91,
    93, 95
Certeau, Michel de, xxii
Champney, Katharina, 84
chaplaincy, ix–x, xxi, xxvi, 1–16
Christ, 15, 37, 48–50, 58–59, 63–64,
    68, 71–72, 96
church, xviii, xxiv, 7–9, 11–13, 17,
    20–21, 23–24, 26, 28, 33, 38,
    40, 42, 45, 48, 50, 64, 70–71,
    84, 91, 98
Citizenship Education, 81
city, xxiii, 33
civil rights movement, xxvii, 7, 76–87
Clark, Septima, xxvii, 76–87
Clayton, Marc, xxi

111

Index

colonialism, 50, 77
community, x, xviii, xxiii, 6, 28, 73, 77–80, 86, 89, 92–94
confidentiality, 90, 94–95
conflict, 80, 90, 92–94
Conjectures of a Guilty Bystander (Merton), xvii
contemplation, 7, 31–33, 37, 43, 50–51, 57, 59, 61–62, 64, 67, 70, 80, 83, 85, 90
Contemplation in a World of Action (Merton), xxvi
contemplative and prophetic perspective, ix, 9, 15–16, 30, 41, 46, 52, 96
cosmos, 57, 60, 63, 67, 74
Cotton, Dorothy F., 78
Creaner, Mary, 49
creation, 41, 58–60, 62–63, 67–71, 74–75
culture, xxiii, 7, 10, 19, 24, 33, 40, 46, 50, 81, 86

Dalai Lama, 2, 82
Daly, Mary, 72, 77
Dancing in the Water of Life (Merton), xx, xxvii
Day, Dorothy, 2
Dear, John, 90, 94
death, 19, 21–23, 48
deer, 65
Delp, Alfred, 77
desert mothers and fathers, 33–37
Dewey, John, 78–79
displaced persons, 21–22, 24
Doherty, Katherine de Hueck, 2

ecology, xxiii, 2, 17, 76
ecology of faith, 21–22, 25, 28
education, ix–x, xix, xxiii, 2, 5, 29–30, 78–81, 83, 86, 88–96, 99
Elliott, John H., 22
eschatology, 31, 49
Eucharist, 93, 95

Evagrius Ponticus, xxvi, 58, 61–62, 64, 71
Evdokimov, Paul, 66, 70

feminist theology, 40, 71, 76–77
Foucault, Michel, 60
Fromm, Erich, 2, 82

Gandhi, Mahatma, 50, 77–78
Germany, xxiii, xxvi, 53
God, 11–15, 18, 23–27, 32, 34, 36–37, 40–43, 45–47, 50–52, 58–64, 67–71, 85
Graham, Elaine, xxi
Gregory of Nyssa, 64

Harding, Vincent, 77–78, 91
Hausherr, Irénée, 57, 71
healthcare, 3–10, 89, 95
Heschel, Abraham Joshua, 2, 82
Highlander Folk School, 82–84
Holy Spirit, 34, 50
hooks, bell, 77, 80, 89–90, 92–94
Horan, Daniel, xxiv
humility, 15, 36, 42

incarnation, 49–50, 58, 71
The Inner Experience (Merton), 61
Intergroup Dialogue, 89–95
An Introduction to Christian Mysticism (Merton), xxvi, 57, 61–63
Islam, 4, 14, 16, 27, 47

Jägerstätter, Franz, 77
Jenkins, Ruth, 1
Juliana of Norwich, 18

Kehoe, Deborah, 53
Kern, Kyprian, xxvii, 54, 66–69, 75
King, Martin Luther Jr., 77, 80–82, 91

ladder and ascent imagery, 54, 70, 74

Index

Lartey, Emmanuel, 19
Latin America, 50
lay people, 5, 54, 64, 70, 74
Leach, Jane, xxiii, 30–52
lectio divina, xviii
Levinas, Emmanuel, xxi
liberation theology, 40
liturgy, 32, 47, 60, 62, 67–68, 73
logos, 58, 60, 62, 68, 71
Loobuyck, Patrick, 4
Lossky, Vladimir, 56–57
Louth, Andrew, 60

Malcolm X, 80
Marcuse, Herbert, 12, 27
marginality, 5, 11, 14, 20–23, 28, 37, 39, 50, 81, 87, 92
Maritain, Jacques, 2, 79–80
Maritain, Raïssa, 18
Massignon, Louis, 2, 24
maturity, ix, xxi, xxii, 35, 42–43, 64, 84–85
Maximus the Confessor, xxvii, 54–75, 77
Meade, Mark, 21
Merton, Owen, 1
Merton, Thomas
    biography, xxi, 1–3, 79
    calligraphies, xx
    contemplative activist, 89
    guilty bystander, 21
    hermit, xx, 2, 45, 65
    interreligious dialogue, 24, 27, 33, 54, 63–64, 74, 76
    lecturer, 2, 96
    letter writer, 28, 34, 96
    master of novices, xix–xx, 2, 28, 34, 37, 47, 57, 96
    master of scholastics, xix–xx, 57, 96
    ministry of friendship, xx, 34, 63, 74
    monk, xix–xx, xxv, 1, 11, 17, 20–24, 28, 32, 34–35, 37, 40, 45, 96, 97–100

mystical-prophetic approach, xxii, 37, 75, 96
organizer of retreats, 7–9, 28, 34, 96–97
pastoral course, xviii, xxvi, 57, 61
pastoral ministry, xix–xxi, xxiv
pastoral practitioner, xix, xxv, 35, 45, 96
prayer, xix, 10, 18, 25, 46–47, 52, 98–99
reading, xxv, 3, 35, 54, 56–57, 59, 69, 74
research, xx, 99
spiritual director, xix–xx, 34–35, 96
vocation, xix, xxv, 40–41, 46, 86, 96, 98–99
writer, xvii–xviii, 1, 89, 96, 98
Meyendorf, John, 66
migration, x, xxvi, 3, 12–13, 16, 17–28, 90
Miles, Margaret, xxv, 19
Miller, Henry, 2
Milosz, Czeslaw, 2
Muslim, x, 3 5, 12, 14, 16, 24, 27, 63, 74
mystical-prophetic approach, ix, xxi–xxii, 37, 75, 96
mysticism, ix–x, xxi–xxii, xxvi, 24, 32, 37, 61–63, 67, 71, 75, 80, 85, 92, 96

Nasr, Sayyed Hossein, 2
natural contemplation, 53–75
nature, xx, 44, 46, 50, 54, 56, 60–62, 65, 68, 72, 89
The New Man (Merton), 59
New Seeds of Contemplation (Merton), xviii
Nhất Hạnh, Thích, 2, 77, 82, 91
nonbelievers, 39, 50, 82–84
nonviolence, 15, 31, 49–51, 77
Nouwen, Henri, 2
Nussbaum, Martha, xxv, 19

Index

Ocampo, Victoria, 2
Orthodox pastoral theology, 66–75
Oyer, Gordon, xxvii, 88–96

Palamas, Gregory, 66–67
Palmer, Parker J., 32
paradise, 59, 63–64
Paris, xxvi, 1, 57, 66, 75
parish, xxiii, 99
Parks, Rosa, 82
Pasternak, Boris, 2
pastoral care, ix, xxi, xxiii, 6, 9–10, 13, 15–16, 28, 48, 89
pastoral ministry, 66–67
pastoral practice, xxvi, 49, 68
pastoral supervision, ix–x, xxvi, 29–52
Paterson, Michael, 30–52
patristic tradition, 32, 48, 59–60, 63, 66–68, 71, 74–75
peace activists, xxi, 24, 27–28, 50, 70, 88, 95
Pembroke, Neil, xxii
Phan, Peter C., 27
pilgrimage, xx
Poks, Małgorzata, 53
Pope John XXIII, xx, 2
Pope Paul VI, 2
poverty, 2, 50, 76
power, 10–12, 20–22, 26–28, 33, 39, 42, 45, 50–51, 58, 61, 77–78, 86, 89, 92, 94
practical theology, ix–x, xxi–xxii, 17–28
priesthood, 11, 20, 57, 69, 72–75
priests of creation, 60, 70–71, 74–75
privilege, xxvii, 5, 7, 11, 14, 16, 23, 78, 86, 89, 92
prophetic, ix–x, xvii, xxi–xxii, 8–10, 12, 15–16, 26–28, 30, 33, 37–38, 41, 46, 52, 69, 75–76, 86, 90, 96
Protestant, xxi, 1, 5, 7, 24, 79, 90–91, 93, 95

Pseudo-Dionysius the Areopagite, 67
psychotherapy, 13, 44–45

racism, xxvii, 12, 50, 81
Ruether, Rosemary Radford, 2

Schipani, Daniel S., ix–xi
Schmemann, Alexander, 66
sciences, xxiii, 4, 33, 55, 61
Seeds of Contemplation (Merton), 84–85
self, ix, xxi–xxii, xxiv, 14, 19, 29, 31, 36, 41–42, 46–48, 59–60, 69, 78–79, 92, 95
The Seven Story Mountain (Merton), xxi
sexism, 50
Sheldrake, Philip F., xxii
Snyder, Susanna, xxvi, 18–28
social justice allies, xxvii, 88–96
society, xxv, 3–4, 7–12, 16, 20, 26–28, 33, 35, 38–39, 41, 45, 48, 50, 56, 61, 73, 77, 86–87, 92
South Africa, 46–47
spiritual care, 6
spiritual community, 28
spiritual direction, xviii, xx, xxvi, 33–34, 43–44, 99
The Springs of Contemplation (Merton), xxvi, 15
Sufism, 14, 27, 47
Suzuki, Daisetz T., 54, 63, 74, 82

technology, xxvi, 2, 11, 56, 61, 76
theological reflection, ix, xxi, xxiii–xxv, 32, 37, 40, 46–47, 49
theoria physike, 61–63, 71
Thoughts in Solitude (Merton), xviii
Thunberg, Lars, 57
Thurston, Bonnie, 9
Tobin, Mary Luke, xix, 76, 78
Tracy, David, xxii
transformation, xxvi, 31, 47–49, 51–52, 86

Index

transnationalism, 28 69, 77–78, 80, 86–87
Trible, Phyllis, 22
Trinity, 38, 58, 71
tropos, 62

United Kingdom, xxi, xxiii, 2, 21, 28, 46
United States, 1–2, 11, 28, 81, 99

Veling, Terry A., xxi
violence, 21, 28, 50

Walton, Heather, xxi
Ward, Frances, xxi
Waugh. Evelyn, 2
Weil, Simone, xx, xxii, 77

Weld, Nicki, 48
Williams, Rowan, 32
Wolfteich, Claire, xxii
women, xxiv, 23, 54, 64, 70–75, 76–77, 81, 87, 90
world, xix, 2–3, 11–13, 20–21, 26, 28, 31, 39–40, 45, 51, 54, 58–59, 61, 63–64, 67–69, 73–74, 77–78, 80, 84–87, 98
Wu, John, xvii

Yungblut, June, 77

Zen, 63–64, 74
Zen and the Birds of Appetite (Merton), 63

www.ingramcontent.com/pod-product-compliance
Lightning Source LLC
Chambersburg PA
CBHW072154160426
43197CB00012B/2382